T0194632

ISAIAH 26:3-4

"PERFECT PEACE XIX"

Eyes

VANESSA RAYNER

authorHOUSE®

AuthorHouse™
1663 Liberty Drive
Bloomington, IN 47403
www.authorhouse.com
Phone: 1 (800) 839-8640

Published by AuthorHouse 08/15/2019

ISBN: 978-1-7283-2356-5 (sc)
ISBN: 978-1-7283-2355-8 (e)

Library of Congress Control Number: 2019912172

Print information available on the last page.

This book is printed on acid-free paper.

The Scriptures' quotations are taken from the KJV, ASV, DARBY, DRA, and WEB.

The King James Version present on the Bible Gateway matches the
1987 printing. The KJV is public domain in the United States.

Douay-Rheims Version present on the Bible Gateway is in the public domain.
It is a translation of the Bible from the Latin Vulgate into English made by
members of the Catholic seminary English College, Douai, France. Is the
foundation on which nearly all English Catholic versions are still based.

Darby Translation present on the Bible Gateway is in the public domain. John
Nelson Darby was converted in his twenties. He was an Anglo-Irish Bible
teacher, one of the influential figures among the original Plymouth Brethren.

American Standard Version present on the Bible Gateway is in the public
domain. It is a revision of the King James Version and was released in 1901.

World English Bible present on the Bible Gateway is a public
domain. It is an updated revision of the American Standard
Version of the Holy Bible first published in 1901.

CONTENTS

A Gift..vii
Theme ix
Prayer xi
Author's Notes..xiii
Preface...xix
Thanks xxi
Acknowledgements xxiii
Introduction xxv
Dedication... xxvii

Chapter 1   OOH My God!..1
Chapter 2   The First Book...7
Chapter 3   The 2nd, 3rd, and 4th Books of the Law ... 17
Chapter 4   The Last Book of the Law 26
Chapter 5   Joshua, Judges & Ruth 33
Chapter 6   The Books of 1st and 2nd Samuel............. 40
Chapter 7   The Books of 1st and 2nd Kings............... 48
Chapter 8   The Books of 1st and 2nd Chronicles 55
Chapter 9   Ezra, Nehemiah & Esther......................... 61
Chapter 10   The 1st Poetic Book 67
Chapter 11   Lyrical Poems.. 73
Chapter 12   To Be Like... 82
Chapter 13   The Last Two Poetic Books 88
Chapter 14   The Book of Isaiah...................................... 94
Chapter 15   The Books of Jeremiah & Lamentations.. 103
Chapter 16   The Last Two Major Prophet Books........ 112
Chapter 17   The Minor Prophet Books 121
Chapter 18   The Synoptic Gospels 130
Chapter 19   Acts of the Apostles 136

Chapter 20   The Epistles of Paul 143
Chapter 21   The Leader of the Early Church.............. 149
Chapter 22   John the Apostle....................................... 156
A Reader's Question... 165

Author's Closing Remarks... 167
References 169
Answers & Information Section 173
Other Books by the Author... 183

A GIFT

*P*resented to

_____

*F*rom

_____

*D*ate

_____

The eyes of Jehovah are toward the righteous,
And his ears are open unto their cry . . . .
Psalm 34:15 ASV

THEME

The message of **Isaiah 26:3-4** is "Perfect Peace." This message is the distinct and unifying composition of this book with the subtitle "Eyes."

A Song of Praise

There are four Bible Translations that I came across in writing my last book that is in the public domain. In honor of those four Translations, the theme message of this book will be stated in those translations below.

Thou wilt keep him in perfect peace, whose mind is stayed on thee; because he trusteth in thee. Trust ye in Jehovah for ever; for in Jehovah, even Jehovah, is an everlasting rock.

Isaiah 26:3 – 4 ASV

Thou wilt keep in perfect peace the mind stayed [on thee], for he confideth in thee. Confide ye in Jehovah for ever; for in Jah, Jehovah, is the rock of ages.

Isaiah 26:3 – 4 Darby

The old error is passed away: thou will keep peace: peace, because we have hoped in thee. You have hoped in the Lord for evermore, in the Lord God mighty for ever.

Isaiah 26:3 – 4 DRA

You will keep whoever's mind is steadfast in perfect peace, because he trusts in you. Trust in Yahweh forever; for in Yah, Yahweh, is an everlasting Rock.

Isaiah 26:3 – 4 WEB

PRAYER

Oh, Heavenly Father,
I thank you for another day. I thank
you for another day on earth.
Father, you been good to me. You
been good to me! Hallelujah!
I pray that your people and their families are being bless.

Oh, Heavenly Father,
I ask in Jesus' name that the Holy Spirit
will help readers to remember
and take heart to Your word.
I pray the word of God will give
them peace, in all situations.
Thank you, Father, for blessing those
that help Your work go forth.

Oh, Heavenly Father,
Your word made it clear that You will
reward those that bless your servant.
It could be through prayer, words of
encouragement, to giving that person
a cup of water.

Mark 9:41 states,
For whosoever shall give you a cup of water to drink
in [my] name because ye are Christ's, verily I say unto
you, he shall in no wise lose his reward; Darby.

Oh, Heavenly Father,
I give you all the Glory, Honor, and Praise in Jesus' name.

Amen.

AUTHOR'S NOTES

Author's notes generally provide a way to add extra information to one's book that may be awkward and inappropriate to include in the text of the book itself. It offers supplemental contextual details on the aspects of the book. It can help readers understand the book content and the background details of the book better. The times and dates of researching, reading, and gathering this information are not included; mostly when I typed on it.

1528; Thursday, 25 April 2019; This morning at 0644, after hitting snooze twice, I started getting ready for work, and my right eye was jumping, like crazy; my left eye had been jumping all last week. I checked my blood pressure, and it was normal. I looked closely at the whites of my eyes because of the incident that happened to my left eye last month, and they were still white. I asked Father God was something good going to happen to me because the old wise saying says, "if your eye is jumping, something good is going to happen." I laughed at myself and asked Father what in the world is going on with my eye. Shortly after, I thought to myself, and said within my heart, "that's a good title for a book, isn't it Father?" I then wrote the time on the calendar and kept getting ready for work.

0504; Saturday, 27 April 2019

0714; Sunday, 28 April 2019

0825; Sunday, 05 May 2019

1705; Monday, 06 May 2019

1903; Monday, 13 May 2019

1823; Tuesday, 14 May 2019

1611; Wednesday; 15 May 2019; Started New Schedule 0700 – 1530. Hallelujah!

0624; Saturday, 18 May 2019

0524; Sunday, 19 May 2019

1613; Monday, 20 May 2019

1912; Tuesday, 21 May 2019

2025; Wednesday, 22 May 2019

0427; Saturday, 25 May 2019

2004; Sunday, 26 May 2019

0550; Monday, 27 May 2019; Happy Memorial Day!

2028; Wednesday, 29 May 2019

1825; Thursday, 30 May 2019

0759; Saturday; 01 Jun. 2019

0620; Sunday, 02 June 2019

1823; Monday, 03 June 2019

1838; Tuesday, 04 June 2019

1558; Wednesday, 05 June 2019

0704; Thursday, 06 June 2019; I'm waiting on Conway Services this morning concerning my hot water tank. An excellent time to take advantage of the day off, to work on this book, in spite of the situation. God is Worthy to be praised. Hallelujah! I believe I'm going to look over and work on Chapter 12, for a tap.

0623; Friday, 07 June 2019; Conway will be replacing the hot water tank, today. By the way, yesterday around 1300 hours, I decide to go to Subway to get something to eat. When I returned to my car, it wouldn't start. It gave me a message concerning the anti-thief immobilizer. I walked home, and later that evening, I had it towed to Ford Motor Company on Moriah St. Praise the LORD! I asked Father God, "what do you want me to learn from this?" Hallelujah!

0609; Saturday, 08 June 2019

0556; Sunday, 09 June 2019

1812; Monday, 10 June 2019

1846; Tuesday, 11 June 2019

1924; Wednesday, 12 June 2019

1817; Thursday, 13 June 2019

0553; Sunday, 16 June 2019; Happy Father Day in RIP, Rev. Ambous Lee Moore

1943; Tuesday, 18 June 2019

0627; Saturday, 22 June 2019

0650; Sunday, 23 June 2019

1939; Monday, 24 June 2019

1845; Tuesday, 25 June 2019

1858; Wednesday, 26 June 2019

2116; Friday, 28 June 2019

0717; Saturday, 29 June 2019

0523; Sunday, 30 June 2019

1809; Monday, 01 July 2019

1801; Wednesday, 03 July 2019

0539; Thursday, 04 July 2019; Happy 4th of July

1717; Friday, 05 July 2019

0656; Saturday, 06 July 2019

0600; Sunday, 07 July 2019; I'm going do a little more proofreading.

1858; Tuesday, 09 July 2019; Happy Birthday Son ~ Alvin

1745; Thursday, 11 July 2019

1631; Friday, 12 July 2019

0729; Saturday, 13 July 2019

2017; Sunday, 14 July 2019

2130; Sunday, 14 July 2019; About to send manuscript to AuthorHouse in a few minutes. Hallelujah!

2041; Tuesday, 16 July 2019; AuthorHouse requested that I make some adjustments, alterations, and/or amendments to the book.

1900; Wednesday, 17 July 2019

1950; Thursday, 18 July 2019

1211; Friday, 19 July 2019; Happy Birthday Mom ~ Ulyer Moore

1609; Saturday, 20 July 2019

0531; Sunday, 21 July 2019

1843; Monday, 22 July 2019

1941; Tuesday, 23 July 2019

0000; Wednesday, 24 July 2019

1719; Thursday, 25 July 2019

1642; Friday, 26 July 2019; Happy Birthday Sister ~ Regina Moore

0000; Saturday, 27 July 2019

0057; Sunday, 28 July 2019

1820; Monday, 29 July 2019

1812; Tuesday, 30 July 2019

1651; Wednesday, 31 July 2019 ~ I am enjoying Bro. James's prayer line from Georgia. In attendance is Bro. Miller from Arkansas, Sister Barbara from Atlanta, and me. My soul is truly being blessed. I briefly spoke on the "Prince of Peace." Hallelujah! At this time, we have never met or seen each other.

1309; Friday, 02 August 2019

0545; Saturday, 03 August 2019

0726; Sunday, 04 August 2019; Internet down . . .

1659; Monday, 05 August 2019; Internet down . . . I'm still going to read over and work on. Internet supposed to be fix by tomorrow.

2026; Tuesday, 06 August 2019; Internet still down.

1624; Wednesday, 07 August 2019; Internet up. Praise God!

1633; Thursday, 08 August 2019

1624; Friday, August 09, 2019

0657; Saturday, August 10, 2019

1156; Saturday, 10 August 2019; About to sent the revised manuscript to AuthorHouse.

PREFACE

Isaiah 26:3-4, "Perfect Peace XIX" Eyes

The book <u>Isaiah 26:3-4, "Perfect Peace XIX" Eyes</u> is the 19th book in a series called Isaiah 26:3-4, "Perfect Peace." Hallelujah!

It all started from how I drew near to the LORD in my workplace by keeping my mind on Him. I related numbers you see throughout the day, everywhere, on almost everything on Him, His word, biblical events, and facts to give me peace in the midst of chaos.

It's our desire for you to discover the power of the Holy Spirit by numbers, words, places, people, and things surrounding the word "eyes."

Remember, the LORD Jesus <u>PROMISED us TRIBULA-TION</u> while we were in this world.

These things, I have spoken unto you,
that in me ye might have peace.
In the world ye shall have tribulation:
But be of good cheer; I have overcome the world.
John 16:33 KJV

However, we have been <u>PROMISED His PEACE</u> while we endure these trials, tribulations, troubles, and tests. Perfect Peace is given only to those whose mind and heart reclines upon the LORD. God's peace is increased in us according to the knowledge of His Holy Word.

> **Grace and peace be multiplied unto you
> through the knowledge of God,
> and of Jesus our LORD.**
> 2 Peter 1:2 KJV

THANKS

To the Readers of the World

As a disciple of the LORD Jesus Christ, I have learned true success comes when we are seeking and striving to do God's purpose for our lives. Our real happiness lies in doing God's will; not in fame and fortune.

I appreciate your support. Thanks for helping me spread the "Perfect Peace Series" through your e-mail, Facebook, Twitter, LinkedIn, Instagram, Tumblr, Messenger or other accounts to your family, friends, neighbors, co-workers, church family, internet social friends, and associates.

Remember, you may not know until you get to heaven just how much a song you sung, kind words spoken by you, a book you suggested reading, or gave as a gift, at the right moment, encourage that person to keep on going when a few minutes before they were tempted to give up on life and their walk with the LORD.

Your lovingkindness to this ministry is greatly appreciated.

ACKNOWLEDGEMENTS

Writing a book is truly, harder than I thought, and more rewarding than I could have ever imagined. I wish to express my sincere gratitude to "Our Heavenly Father" for his guidance, patience, and lovingkindness throughout the writing of this book.

I want to express my appreciation to AuthorHouse Check-In Coordinator, for her endless support, thoughtfulness, and understanding during this process; RT.

To my sons, who in one way, or another shared their support, either verbally, morally, financially, or physically, thank you.

I'm grateful to my prayer line families whom I worship with, pray with, study the word with and talk with. You all bless my soul more than you will ever know. May the Almighty richly bless all of you!

INTRODUCTION

For Those Who Want to Be Kept In "Perfect Peace"

This book titled, <u>Isaiah 26:3 – 4, "Perfect Peace XIX" Eyes</u> was prepared and written to open your mind to a "Perfect Peace" that comes only from God. I'm striving through this book to elevate you into a "Unique and Profound" awareness of God's presence around you at all time.

According to some people, it's hard to keep your mind on the LORD. While most Christians will agree that if you keep your mind stayed on the LORD, He will keep you in "Perfect Peace." Therefore, so many people enjoy going to church on Sundays and attending midweek services for the peace and joy that they receive; but only for a short time.

You can experience the peace of the LORD throughout the day and every day. His unspeakable joy, his strength, his "Perfect Peace" during the storm whether it's at work, home, college, school, etc. You can also experience this peace, even when your day is going well.

This concept of this book was placed in my spirit by our Father, which art in heaven, to help me when he allowed Satan to test me at my workplace until he finished molding me into a MAP; (Minister/Ambassador/Pastor).

Throughout these pages, I will be focussing on biblical events, and facts surrounding the word "eyes." However, I am sure much more can be said concerning "eyes" in the Bible, so these chapter subjects serve merely as an introduction and are not exhaustive by any means.

DEDICATION

Ophthalmologists, Optometrists, Orthoptists, and Opticians, this book is dedicated to you. May the LORD keep you as the apple of His eye.

The branch of medicine that specializes in the anatomy, function, diseases and surgical care of the eyes is called Ophthalmology.

An Ophthalmologist specializes in the surgical care of the eyes; as well as the prevention of eye diseases and disorders.

An Optometrist examines the eyes for visual defects and diagnose problems. This individual prescribes corrective lenses and provides certain types of eye treatment.

An Orthoptist is a certified health care professional who works under the supervision of an Ophthalmologist to evaluate and treat disorders of the eyes.

An Optician is a health care professional who is trained to prepare and dispense optical appliances for the eyes based on written prescriptions. An Optician shapes and finishes the eyeglass lenses and frames.

CHAPTER 1

OOH MY GOD!

The Bible is recognized as having around 31,103 verses, depending on the Bible translation. The top-selling English Bible translations in the United States are NIV, KJV, NLT, NKJV, and ESV. The Bible translations belong to 1 of 3 translation types, which are called formal equivalence, functional equivalence, and dynamic equivalence. **PS:** More information on formal, functional, and dynamic equivalence is in the back of the book taken from the book titled: <u>Isaiah 26:3-4 "Perfect Peace" The Last Single Digit</u>. It was published on 02/15/2012.

The Bible has been translated into approximately 700 languages from the biblical languages of Hebrew, Aramaic, and Greek. The Old Testament was written primarily in Hebrew on scrolls between 1500 and 400 BC. Scholars believe that parts of Daniel, Ezra, and Jeremiah were written in Aramaic. The New Testament is believed to have been written in Greek.

Note of Interests: Aramaic was spread by the Babylonian's Empire. Jesus lived and spent most of his time in the towns of Nazareth and Capernaum in Galilee, which were Aramaic-speaking people.

The Bible has over 40 writers and is compiled of writings that cover approximately 1400 years. Moses was the first person to write portions of the Bible, and John, the disciple of Jesus, wrote the last part. Others well-known writers of the Bible include Ezra, Nehemiah, David, Solomon, Isaiah, Jeremiah, Ezekiel, Daniel, Hosea, Joel, Amos, Obadiah, Jonah, Micah, Nahum, Habakkuk, Zephaniah, Haggai, Zechariah, Malachi, Matthew, Mark, Luke, Paul, Peter, James, and Jude. The Bible is the history of God's creation, His involvement, interaction, and His future plans with humanity.

Note of Interests: All other history books record and speak on the past, only. Beginning in Genesis 1, the Bible records the history of humanity from the beginning, and Revelation 21 records the future history of humanity when the day the earth will pass away, and a new heaven and new earth will appear.

The King James Version of the Bible has 66 books, 1189 chapter, 31,3102 verses, and 31,3102 verses. The word "eyes" is recorded in the KJV Bible 502 times in 479 verses in the KJV Bible; 408 in the Old Testament, and 71 in the New Testament.

The Old Testament begins with the creation of the heaven, and the earth by God, and ends with the Persian ruling over Israel around 425 BC. Then 400 years passed from the writing of the last book of the Old Testament to the birth of Christ in the New Testament. Scholars refer to those years as the silent years, the years in which God did not speak, nor speak through his prophets.

The word "eyes" is mentioned twice in some of the verses beginning with Genesis 41:37, Genesis 45:12, Exodus 5:21, Deuteronomy 3:27, 1 Samuel 26:24, 2 Kings 4:34, 2 Kings 6:17, 2 Kings 6:20, 2 Kings 25:7, Song of Solomon 5:12, Isaiah 6:10, Jeremiah 16:17, Jeremiah 32:4, Jeremiah 34:3, Ezekiel 8:5, Daniel 7:8, Zechariah 8:6, Matthew 13:15, Matthew 20:34, John 12:40, and Acts 28:27. Psalm 123:2 is the only verse in the Bible where the word "eyes" is mentioned 3 times in a single verse; that particular verse contains 42 words.

Note of Interests: Psalm 123 has only 4 verses that contain 94 words. It is one of the 15 psalms that begins with the words "A Song of Ascents." Psalm 123 is Psalm 122 in the Greek Septuagint version of the Bible, and in its Latin translation in the Vulgate. Psalm 123 is a prayer for mercy with our eyes looking to the LORD for compassion in our time of affliction. Pilgrims sing this Psalms on their way to Jerusalem at feast time.

In the Old Testament, the word "eyes" is mentioned the most in the books of Psalms (42), Genesis (37), and Isaiah (36). In the New Testament, the word "eyes" is mentioned the most in the books of John (17), Matthew (10), and Luke and Revelation (9).

Note of Interests: The word "eye" without the "s" is mentioned in 93 verses in the KJV Bible; 70 in the Old Testament, and 23 in the New Testament. In the Old Testament, the word "eye" is mentioned the most in the books of Job (13), Psalms (11), and Deuteronomy (10). In the

New Testament, the word "eye" is mentioned in only 5 books which are Matthew (10), Mark (3), Luke (4), 1 Corinthians (5) and Revelation (1).

In the KJV Bible, the word "eyes" is not mentioned in the following books:

Old Testament:	New Testament:
1. Obadiah	1 Corinthians
2. Jonah	2 Corinthians
3. Nahum	Philippians
4.	1 Thessalonians
5.	2 Thessalonians
6.	1 Timothy
7.	2 Timothy
8.	Titus
9.	Philemon
10.	James
11.	1 John
12	2 John
13.	Jude

PS: Let me take a break to pray, fast, and seek Father God's face on how to proceed; 0806 on 04/28/2019.

The eyes are part of the organs of the visual system. The visual system is part of the central nervous system that acts as a receiver and processor of information. The eyes, optic nerve, optic chiasm, optic tract, lateral geniculate nucleus, optical radiation, visual cortex, and visual association cortex are part of the visual system.

The human eyes are the most complex organs next to the brain. The eyes detect light from the environment and allow vision to occur with the help of 7 essential components.

The outermost layer of the eye is called the cornea. The cornea allows light to pass into the interior of the eyes, focuses it, then allows the light to reach the lens and retina. The cornea is the clear smooth covering on the surface portion of the eye. It protects the eyes from dust and particles.

The pupil is the black circular opening in the middle of the iris. The pupil acts as a guardian. It monitors and controls the amount of light hitting the retina. The pupil will contract when there is too much light to keep from damaging the retina.

The iris is the colored part of the eye. The iris adjusts the size of the pupil by contracting or expanding its muscles when the pupil needs to process an image.

The lens exists behind the pupil. It is responsible for allowing the eyes to focus on small details, like words in a book. In old age, the lens cannot adjust well to its surrounding as it used to and become opaque, a condition known as a cataract.

The vitreous humour encompasses a large portion of the eyeball. It is a jelly-like substance that occupies the space behind the lens and in front of the retina at the back of the eyes. It helps to keep the eyeball in its proper, circular shape.

In old age, the vitreous humour begins to shrink, which can lead to permanent vision loss.

Note of Interests: Isaac, Israel and Eli eyes waxed dim in old age according to Genesis 27:1, Genesis 48:10, and 1 Samuel 4:15.

─❧❀❧─

The layer of tissue in the back of the eye, which is located near the optic nerve is called the retina. The retina receives the refined, visual message from the front of the eye, and then transmits that message to the brain using electrical signals.

The sclera is the part of the eyes, known as the "white." It is the white part of the eyes, and it provides strength, structure, lubricate, and protects the eyes. It forms the supporting wall of the eyeballs. The sclera has blood vessels which can tell an eye-doctor the overall condition of your health.

> **The lamp of the body is the eye.**
> **If therefore your eye is sound, your**
> **whole body will be full of light.**
> Matthew 6:22 WEB

CHAPTER 2

THE FIRST BOOK

Genesis is the 1ˢᵗ book of the Bible with 50 chapters. It is also considered the 1ˢᵗ of the 5 books of Moses. The other books of Moses are Exodus, Leviticus, Numbers, and Deuteronomy, and these books are often called "The Law of Moses." Pentateuch is another name the 5 books of Moses are called, which means "5 scrolls." These books are also called Torah by scholars, which means "to guide" or "teach."

The Book of Genesis is about beginnings, and it covers at least 2,200 years, and possibly many more. It can be divided and outlined in several different formats, ways, and viewpoints. Scholars divide the Book of Genesis into 2 sections, chapters 1 – 11, creation and fallen man, and chapters 12 – 50, God's patriarchs and redemption for man. However, Genesis can be outlined and narrow down as follow:

Chapters 1 – 2   Creation
Chapters 3 – 5   Man Fall
Chapters 6 – 9   The Flood
Chapters 10 – 11   The Tower of Babel
Chapters 12 – 25   Abraham
Chapters 25 – 26   Isaac
Chapters 27 – 36   Jacob
Chapters 37 – 50   Joseph

According to the teachings of the Abrahamic religion, Moses was a prophet. His father was Amram, and his mother was Jochebed. Moses was born during the time when the Israelites were slaves in Egypt. The King had issued a decreed that the midwives were to kill all Hebrews boys when they were born, leaving only the girl babies alive.

Moses' mother hid Moses in a basket and set him afloat on the Nile River to save his life. Pharaoh's daughter found Moses in the basket, and she took pity on him, adopting him as her child, Exodus 2. Moses was adopted by the Egyptian princess when he was a baby, and later in life became the leader of the Israelites at age 80 and lawgiver.

Throughout the Bible, the writers of scripture use the image and likeness of "eyes" in various ways, fashions, and descriptions. The reference to "eyes" is mentioned 39 times in 37 verses in the first book of the Bible. The reference to "eyes" is listed below in the KJV with a subject title.

Man Fall

The Fall of Adam and Eve, Genesis 3:1 – 24
For God doth know that in the day ye eat thereof, then your eyes shall be opened, and ye shall be as gods, Genesis 3:5.

Note of Interests: Eve was named by her husband, Adam. Adam named her "Eve" because she became the mother of all who lived, Genesis 3:20. Adam also named all the animals. God named Adam, and his name means "earth." God created Adam out of the dust of the ground, and God created Eve from one of Adam's ribs.

And when the woman saw that the tree was good for food and that it was pleasant to the eyes, and a tree to be desired to make one wise, she took of the fruit thereof, and did eat, and gave also unto her husband with her; and he did eat, Genesis 3:6.

And the eyes of them both were opened, and they knew that they were naked; and they sewed fig leaves together, and made themselves aprons, Genesis 3:7.

The Flood

The Wickedness of Man, Genesis 6:1 – 8
But Noah found grace in the eyes of the Lord, Genesis 6:8.

Abraham

Abram and Lot Separate, Genesis 13:1 – 18
And Lot lifted up his eyes, and beheld all the plain of Jordan, that it was well watered every where, before the LORD destroyed Sodom and Gomorrah, even as the garden of the LORD, like the land of Egypt, as thou comest unto Zoar, Genesis 13:10.

And the LORD said unto Abram, after that Lot was separated from him, Lift up now thine eyes, and look from the place where thou art northward, and southward, and eastward, and westward, Genesis 13:14.

Sarai and Hagar Drama, Genesis 16:1 – 16
And he went in unto Hagar, and she conceived: and when she saw that she had conceived, her mistress was despised in her eyes, Genesis 16:4.

And Sarai said unto Abram, My wrong be upon thee: I have given my maid into thy bosom; and when she saw that she had conceived, I was despised in her eyes: the LORD judge between me and thee, Genesis 16:5.

Note of Interests: Abraham was 86 years old when Ishmael was born by Sarai's maid, Hagar. Abraham was 100 years old when Isaac was born by his wife, Sarai. Ishmael was around 14 years old when Isaac was born. According to Genesis 25:7, Abraham was 175 years old when he died. Ishmael and Isaac were both at the burial of their father; Ishmael was 89 years old, and Isaac was 75 years old.

<u>The Lord Promises Abraham a Son</u>, Genesis 18:1 – 15
And he lift up his eyes and looked, and, lo, 3 men stood by him: and when he saw them, he ran to meet them from the tent door, and bowed himself toward the ground, Genesis 18:2.

<u>Sodom's Perversion</u>, Genesis 19:1 – 11
Behold now, I have 2 daughters which have not known man; let me, I pray you, bring them out unto you, and do ye to them as is good in your eyes: only unto these men do nothing; for therefore came they under the shadow of my roof, Genesis 19:8.

<u>Abraham, Sarah and Abimelech at Gerar</u>, Genesis 20:1 – 18
And unto Sarah he said, Behold, I have given thy brother 1,000 pieces of silver: behold, he is to thee a covering of the eyes, unto all that are with thee, and with all other: thus she was reproved, Genesis 20:16.

<u>Hagar and Ishamel Sent Away</u>, Genesis 21:8 – 21
And God opened her eyes, and she saw a well of water; and she went, and filled the bottle with water, and gave the lad drink, Genesis 21:19.

<u>Abraham Tested</u>, Genesis 22:1 – 19
Then on the 3rd day Abraham lifted up his eyes, and saw the place afar off, Genesis 22:4.

And Abraham lifted up his eyes, and looked, and behold behind him a ram caught in a thicket by his horns: and Abraham went and took the ram and offered him up for a burnt offering in the stead of his son, Genesis 22:13.

<u>Isaac Marries Rebekah</u>, Genesis 24:1 – 67
And Isaac went out to mediate out to meditate in the field at the eventide: and he lifted up his eyes, and saw, and, behold, the camels were coming, Genesis 24:63.

And Rebekah lifted up her eyes, and when she saw Isaac, she lighted off the camel, Genesis 24:64.

Jacob

<u>Jacob Steals Esau's Blessing</u>, Genesis 27:1 – 40
And it came to pass, that when Isaac was old, and his eyes were dim, so that he could not see, he called Esau his eldest son, and said unto him, My son: and he said unto him, Behold, here am I, Genesis 27:1.

Jacob's Flocks Increase, Genesis 30:25 – 43

And Laban said unto him, I pray thee, if I have found favour in thine eyes, tarry: for I have learned by experience that the Lord hath blessed me for thy sake, Genesis 30:27.

And it came to pass, whensoever the stronger cattle did conceive, that Jacob laid the rods before the eyes of the cattle in the gutters, that they might conceive among the rods, Genesis 30:41.

Jacob Flees from Laban, Genesis 31:1 – 42

And it came to pass at the time that the cattle conceived, that I lifted up mine eyes, and saw in a dream, and, behold, the rams which leaped upon the cattle were ringstraked, speckled, and grisled, Genesis 31:10.

And he said, Lift up now thine eyes, and see, all the rams which leap upon the cattle are ringstraked, speckled, and grisled: for I have seen all that Laban doeth unto thee, Genesis 31:12.

Thus I was; in the day the drought consumed me, and the frost by night; and my sleep departed from mine eyes, Genesis 31:40

Jacob Meets Esau, Genesis 33:1 – 20

And Jacob lifted up his eyes, and looked, and behold, Esau came, and with him 400 men. And he divided the children unto Leah, and unto Rachel, and unto 200 handmaids, Genesis 33:1.

And he lifted up his eyes, and saw the women and the children; and said, Who are those with thee? And he said,

The children which God hat graciously given thy servant, Genesis 33:5.

Dinah's Rape and the Revenge, Genesis 34:1 – 31
And Shechem said unto her father and unto her brethren, Let me find grace in your eyes, and what ye shall say unto me I will give, Genesis 34:11.

Joseph

Joseph Sold into Slavery, Genesis 37:23 – 35
And they sat down to eat bread: and they lifted up their eyes and looked, and behold, a company of Ishmeelites came from Gilead with their camels bearing spicery and balm and myrrh, going to carry it down to Egypt, Genesis 37:25.

Joseph Refuses Potiphar's Wife Sexual Advancement, Genesis 39:7 – 18
And it came to pass after these things, that his master's wife cast her eyes upon Joseph; and she said, Lie with me, Genesis 39:7.

Joseph is Made Governor over Egypt, Genesis 41:37 – 43
And the thing was good in the eyes of Pharaoh, and in the eyes of all his servants, Genesis 41:37.

Joseph's Brothers Goes to Egypt for Grain, Genesis 42:6 – 24
And he turned himself about from them, and wept; and returned to them again, and communed with them, and took from them Simeon, and bound him before their eyes, Genesis 42:24.

<u>Joseph's Brother 2nd Journey to Egypt</u>, Genesis 43:26 – 34
And he lifted up his eyes, and saw his brother Benjamin, his mother's son, and said, Is this your younger brother, of whom ye spake unto me? And he said, God be gracious unto thee, my son, Genesis 43:29.

<u>Judah Pleads for Benjamin</u>, Genesis 44:18 – 34
And thou sadist unto thy servants, Bring him down unto me, that I may set mine eyes upon him, Genesis 44:21.

Remember: Benjamin is Jacob youngest son, his 2nd son by Rachel, but his 12th son; the last son to be born to him. The name "Benjamin" means the "Son of my right hand."

<u>Joseph Reveals Himself to His Brothers</u>, Genesis 45:1 – 28
And, behold, your eyes see, and the eyes of my brother Benjamin, that it is my mouth that speaketh unto you, Genesis 45:12.

<u>Jacob's Journey to Egypt</u>, Genesis 46:1 – 7
I will go down with thee into Egypt; and I will also surely bring thee up again: and Joseph shall put his hand upon thine eyes, Genesis 46:4.

<u>Joseph and the Famine</u>, Genesis 47:1 – 26
Wherefore shall we die before thine eyes, both we and our land? Buy us and our land for bread, and we and our land will be servants unto Pharaoh: and give us seed, that we may live, and not die, that the land be not desolate, Genesis 47:19.

<u>Manasseh and Ephraim</u>, Genesis 48:1 – 22
Now the eyes of Israel were dim for age, so that he could not see. And he brought them near unto him; and he kissed them, and embraced them, Genesis 48:10.

Note of Interests: Manasseh and Ephraim were the grandsons of Jacob (Israel). They were the sons of Joseph, who had been sold into slavery by his brothers when he was about 17 years old. Joseph ends up in the service of an Egyptian official named Potiphar in Egypt. Later, Joseph married his daughter named Asenath, and they have 2 sons; Manasseh the oldest, and Ephraim. Joseph's father, Jacob, was later renamed Israel by God. Israel's 12 tribes and territory division were named after 10 of his sons, and 2 of his grandsons named Ephraim and Manasseh. There was no territory named Levi or Joseph, which are Israel's sons, also. Levi is Jacob (Israel) 3rd son by Leah, and Joseph is his 11th son by Rachel.

<u>Jacob Blesses His Son Judah</u>, Genesis 49:8 – 12
His eyes shall be red with wine, and his teeth white with milk, Genesis 49:12

Remember: Judah was the 4th son of Jacob by Leah. Judah's mother also gave birth to Reuben, Levi, Simeon, Issachar, and Zebulun.

<u>Jacob's Funeral</u>, Genesis 50:1 – 14
And when the days of his mourning were past, Joseph spake unto the house of Pharaoh, saying, If now I have found

grace in your eyes, speak, I pray you, in the ears of Pharaoh, saying, Genesis 50:4.

Note of Interests: The phrase "lifted up his eyes" is mentioned 7 times out of these 37 verses in Genesis. The phrase is only mentioned 20 times in the Bible; 16 in the Old Testament, and 4 times in the New Testament. The phrase "grace in your eyes" is mentioned only twice in the Bible; Genesis 34:11 and Genesis 50:4.

CHAPTER 3

THE 2ND, 3RD, AND 4TH
BOOKS OF THE LAW

The 2nd, 3rd, and 4th books of the "Law of Moses" are Exodus, Leviticus, and Numbers. The word "Exodus" is the Greek word for "departure or going out." The Book of Exodus begins in Egypt and ends at Mount Sinai. Mount Sinai is also known as Mount Horeb, Mountain of Moses, and Mountain of God. This mountain is where Moses saw the burning bush that was not consumed.

The Book of Exodus opens with the names of the sons of Israel who entered Egypt with their household. They were Reuben, Simeon, Levi, Judah, Issachar, Zebulun, Benjamin, Dan, Naphtali, Gad, and Asher. In all, Jacob had 70 descendants in Egypt, including Joseph his son, who was already there.

Note of Interests: The words "sons of Israel" is referring to Jacob's sons. God changed Jacob's name to Israel, Genesis 32:22 – 29. His name was changed after he prevailed at Bethel after wrestling with God all night. The new name was given to establish a new identity.

The Book of Exodus has 40 chapters which gives detail concerning the LORD's call to the people of Israel who were slaves in Egypt. Exodus records their journey through the wilderness to Mount Sinai, led by Moses. It tells of the promises that the LORD made to them concerning the land of Canaan.

Note of Interests: Exodus records more miracles of God than any other book in the Old Testament. The miracles are as follow:

1. The Burning Bush, Exodus 3
2. Aaron's Rod Changed into a Serpent, Exodus 7
3. The Ten Plagues of Egypt, Exodus 7 – 12
4. Red Sea Divided and Israel Passes Through, Exodus 14
5. Waters of Marah is Sweetened in the Wilderness, Exodus 15
6. Manna from Heaven, Exodus 16
7. Water from the Rock at Rephidim, Exodus 17

The word "eyes" is mentioned 7 times in 6 verses in the Book of Exodus. The verses in which the word "eyes" are mentioned are listed below in the American Standard Version (ASV) with a subject title.

Bricks without Straw, Exodus 5:1 – 21
And they said unto them, Jehovah look upon you, and judge; because ye have made our savor to be abhorred in the eyes of Pharaoh, and in the eyes of his servants, to put a sword in their hand to slay us, Exodus 5:21.

The 4th Plague: Flies, Exodus 8:20 – 32
And Moses said, It is not meet so to do; for we shall sacrifice the abomination of the Egyptians to Jehovah our God: lo,

shall we sacrifice the abomination of the Egyptians before their eyes, and will they not stone us? Exodus 8:26.

Dedication of the Firstborn, Exodus 13:1 – 16
And it shall be for a sign unto thee upon thy hand, and for a memorial between thine eyes, that the law of Jehovah may be in thy mouth: for with a strong hand hath Jehovah brought thee out of Egypt, Exodus 13:9.

And it shall be a sign upon thy hand, and for frontlets between thine eyes: for by strength of hand Jehovah brought us forth out of Egypt, Exodus 13:16.

Note of Interests: According to Exodus 13:2, the LORD commands the 1st born male Israelite of each family and every 1st born male beast to be dedicated to Him. The term "firstborn" has two meanings; it relates to the fact when a boy baby is the first to be born to his father. Secondly, it refers to the rights and authority of a son because he is the 1st born. In the Old Testament, the 1st born son usually received a double inheritance and he was the one who would inherit his father's role as head of the family. The rights and authority of the 1st born son have been known to be reversed, changed, and taken away in the Bible. The LORD reversed this order with Jacob and Esau. He told Rebekah there were 2 nations in her womb, but the 1st born who was Esau would serve his brother, Jacob, Genesis 25:21 – 26. Jacob changed the order with his grandsons' Ephraim and Manasseh, Genesis 48:13 – 22. According to Genesis 49:3 – 4, Reuben was the 1st born of Jacob, but his rights were taken away because of his sin; he slept with his father's concubine Bilhah, Genesis 35:22.

The Egyptians Purse Israel, Exodus 14:5 – 14
And when Pharaoh drew nigh, the children of Israel lifted up their eyes, and, behold, the Egyptians were marching after them: and they were sore afraid: and the children of Israel cried out unto Jehovah, Exodus 14:10.

Israel Accepts the Lord's Covenant, Exodus 24:1 – 18
And the appearance of the glory of Jehovah was like devouring fire on the top of the mount in the eyes of the children of Israel, Exodus 24:17.

The Book of Leviticus is the 3rd book in the Old Testament, and it was written between 1440 and 1400 BC. During this time, the Israelites were camped at the foot of Mount Sinai in the desert Peninsula of Sinai.

The Book of Leviticus consists of 27 chapters and around 659 verses. In most of the chapters in Leviticus, God is speaking to Moses; chapters 1 – 7 and 11 – 27. The Book of Leviticus concentrates on God's laws concerning sacrifices, ceremonial laws regarding the priesthood, ceremonial laws concerning purification, laws regarding the sacred feasts and festivals, tithes, offerings, sabbatical and jubilee years.

Note of Interests: The Book of Leviticus speaks on 5 types of offerings. The 5 offerings are the burnt offering, peace offering, meal offering, sin offering, and the trespass offering. There are 613 laws found in the Book of Leviticus.

In the Book of Leviticus, the word "eyes" are mentioned only 3 times in 3 verses, and they are as follow in the Darby Translation with a subject title.

The Sin Offering, Leviticus 4:1 – 35
And if the whole congregation of Israel sin inadvertently, and the thing be hid from the eyes of the congregation, and they do [somewhat against] any of all the commandments of Jehovah [in things] which should not be done, and are guilty; Leviticus 4:13.

Punishments for Those Who Do Not Obey the Law; Sin, Leviticus 20:1 – 27
And if the people of the land do any ways hide their eyes from that man, when he giveth of his seed unto Molech, that they kill him not, Leviticus 20:4.

The Punishment for Being Disobedience, Leviticus 26:14 – 46
I also will do this unto you - I will even appoint over you terror, consumption, and fever, which shall cause the eyes to fail, and the soul to waste away; and ye shall sow your seed in vain, for your enemies shall eat it, Leviticus 26:16.

The Book of Numbers is the 4th book of the Old Testament with 36 chapters. It is also the 4th book of "The Law of Moses." Numbers' name is derived from the 2 censuses that numbered the people of Israel while they were in the wilderness.

The 1st census was taken shortly after the exodus from Egypt, Numbers 26:1 – 2. The census was instructed by Moses and Eleazar the priest on the plains of Moab beside the Jordan River. The leaders of Israel were to list all the men of Israel who were 20 years old and older.

According to Numbers 26, the 2nd census of Israel took place at the end of 40 years in the wilderness. The Israelites were preparing to enter the Promised Land called Canaan. The 2nd census was taken to evaluate Israel's military force. The men who were 20 years old and older, and able to serve in Israel's army were counted. The 1st census count was 603,550 men, and the 2nd count was 601,730. At this time, all of the Israelites who had left Egypt had died except Caleb and Joshua.

Note of Interests: Joshua and Caleb were selected along with 10 other men to spy out Canaan, the Promised Land, Numbers 13. After a 40-day exploration of Canaan, Joshua and Caleb were the only 2 men out of 12 to bring back a good report. They believed God would help them conquer the huge inhabitants of Canaan. They were the only 2 men from their generation permitted to go into the Promised Land after the 40 years of wandering in the wilderness. The 10 men who had brought back a bad report was struck dead with a plague before the LORD, Numbers 14:36 – 38.

In the Book of Numbers, the word "eyes" is mentioned 15 times in 15 verses. They are listed below with a subject title.

<u>An Unfaithful Wife</u>, Numbers 5:11 – 31
And a man lie with her carnally, and it be hid from the eyes of her husband, and be kept close, and she be defiled, and

there be no witness against her, neither she be taken with the manner, Numbers 5:13 KJV.

The Israelites Leave Sinai, Numbers 10:11 – 32
And he said, Leave us not, I pray thee; forasmuch as thou knowest how we are to encamp in the wilderness, and thou mayest be to us instead of eyes, Numbers 10:31 KJV.

Quail from the Lord, Numbers 11:1 – 35
But now our soul is dried away: there is nothing at all, beside this manna, before our eyes, Numbers 11:6 KJV.

Note of Interests: A quail is a small feathered bird that is ordinarily brownish or grayish in color. Quails are considered one of the friendliest birds on earth. They nest on the ground and brood between 12 to 20 eggs. Quail meat cooked is known as being tender, juicy, and delicious. Quail was the LORD provision for the children of Israel when He brought them out of Egypt. The people following Moses complained that they were sick of eating manna every day. The Israelites longed for meat, such as they had back in Egypt, and God heard their grumbling and gave them quail to eat.

Tassels on Garments, Numbers 15:37 – 41
And it shall be unto you for a fringe, that ye may look upon it, and remember all the commandments of the Jehovah, and do them ; and that ye follow not after your own heart and your own eyes, after which ye use to play the harlot; Numbers 15:39 ASV.

The Korah, Dathan, Abiram, and On Rebellion Against Moses,
Numbers 16:1 – 50
Moreover, thou hast not brought us into a land flowing
with milk and honey, nor given us inheritance of fields and
vineyards: wilt thou put out the eyes of these men? We will
not come up, Numbers 16:14 ASV.

Moses Strikes the Rock at Meribah Springs, Numbers 20:1 – 13
Take the rod, and assembly the congregation, thou, and
Aaron thy brother, and speak ye unto the rock before
their eyes, that it give forth its water; and thou shalt bring
forth to them water out of the rock; so thou shalt give the
congregation and their cattle drink, Numbers 20:8 ASV.

Yahweh said to Moses and Aaron, "Because you didn't
believe in me, to sanctify me in the eyes of the children of
Israel, therefore you shall not bring this assembly into the
land which I have given them," Numbers 20:12 WEB.

Balaam Eyes are Opened, Numbers 22:22 – 41
Then Yahweh opened the eyes of Balaam, and he saw
Yahweh's angel standing in the way, and his sword drawn
in his hand; and he bowed his head, and fell flat on his face,
Numbers 22:31 WEB.

Balaam's 3rd Message, Numbers 24:1 – 14
Balaam lifted up his eyes, and he saw Israel dwelling
according to their tribes; and the Spirit of God came upon
him, Numbers 24:2 WEB.

He took up his parable, and said, "Balaam the son of Beor
says, the man whose eyes are open hath said; Numbers
24:3 WEB.

He says, who hears the words of God, who sees the vision of the Almighty, falling down, and having his eyes open: Numbers 24:4 WEB.

Balaam's Last Message, Numbers 24:15 – 25
And he took up his parable, and said, Balaam the son of Beor hath said, and the man whose eyes are open hath said: Numbers 24:15 KJV.

He hath said, which heard the words of God, and knew the knowledge of the most High, which saw the vision of the Almighty, falling into a trance, but having his eyes open: Numbers 24:16 KJV.

Joshua is Appointed Israel's New Leader, Numbers 27:12 – 23
For ye rebelled against my commandment in the desert of Zin, in the strife of the congregation, to sanctify me at the water before their eyes; that is the water of Meribah in Kadesh in the wilderness of Zin, Numbers 27:14 KJV.

Israel at the Border of Canaan, Numbers 33:50 – 56
But if ye will not drive out the inhabitants of the land from before you; then it shall Be pricks in your eyes, and thorns in your sides, and shall vex you in the land wherein ye dwell, Numbers 33:55 KJV.

CHAPTER 4

THE LAST BOOK OF THE LAW

The Book of Deuteronomy is the last book of "The Law of Moses," and it was written around 1407 BC. The Book of Deuteronomy consists of 34 chapters and approximately 959 verses. The word "Deuteronomy" comes from a Greek word that means "second law."

Deuteronomy, chapters 1 through 4 is where Moses repeats the history of the children of Israel, who were once slaves in Egypt to their freedom and wandering in the wilderness. In chapters 5 through 26 of Deuteronomy, Moses repeats the moral law, which is the Ten Commandments; the ceremonial law which govern sacrifices, offerings, and special days; and the civil law which deals with dietary regulations and corporal punishments.

Moses gave 3 speeches to the people of Israel in the plains of Moab before they enter the land of Canaan; the Promised Land. The first speech recounts the 40 years of wandering in the wilderness. The second speech reminds Israel to follow the LORD and His laws. The third speech, Moses tells the nation of Israel even should they be unfaithful to the LORD, if they repent, they can be restored.

The last 4 chapters of Deuteronomy contain the song of Moses, the blessing of Moses, recount the leadership of Moses to Joshua, and the death of Moses on Mount Nebo.

Note of Interests: Mount Nebo is a mountain located in the plains of Moab, on the east side of the Jordan River. Mount Nebo is approximately 2,330 ft. above the Dead Sea' sea level. It was during the final days of Israel's journey to the Promised Land when they camped in Moab near Nebo.

According to the Bible, Mount Nebo is the location where Moses viewed the Promised Land before he died. Moses prayed to God to see the Promised Land, and it was granted.

God did not allow Moses to enter the Promised Land because of what happened at Meribah Kadesh. There God told Moses to speak to the rock, but instead, he struck the rock twice. According to Numbers 20, the Israelites were in the wilderness of Zin, and they were without water. Moses and Aaron prayed, and God told Moses to speak to the rock for water to come forth, but Moses struck it, and water came forth.

Among the 34 chapters in the Book of Deuteronomy, the word "eyes" are mentioned in 30 verses. They are listed below in the King James Version with a short subject title.

Moses Speech to Israel at the Jordan Valley,
Deuteronomy 1:19 – 33
The LORD your God which goeth before you, he shall fight for you, according to all that he did for you in Egypt before your eyes, Deuteronomy 1:30.

<u>Moses Speak to Joshua</u>, Deuteronomy 3:12 – 22
And I commanded Joshua at that time, saying, Thine eyes have seen all that the LORD your God hath done unto these 2 kings: so shall the Lord do unto all the kingdoms whither thou passest, Deuteronomy 3:21.

<u>Moses at Mount Pisgah</u>, Deuteronomy 3:23 – 29
Get thee up into the top of Pisgah, and lift up thine eyes westward, and northward, and southward, and eastward, and behold it with thine eyes: for thou shalt not go over this Jordan, Deuteronomy 3:27.

<u>Moses Urges Israel to Obey</u>, Deuteronomy 4:1 – 14
Your eyes have seen what the LORD did because of Baalpeor: for all the men that followed Baalpeor, the LORD they God hath destroyed them from among you, Deuteronomy 4:3.

Only take heed to thyself, and keep thy soul diligently, lest thou forget the things which thine eyes have seen, and lest they depart from thy heart all the days of thy life: but teach them thy sons, and thy sons' sons, Deuteronomy 4:9.

<u>Moses Warns Against Idolatry</u>, Deuteronomy 4:15 – 31
And lest thou lift up thine eyes unto heaven, and when thou seest the sun, and the moon, and the stars, even all the host of heaven, shouldest be driven to worship them, and serve them, which the LORD thy God hath divided unto all nations under the whole heaven, Deuteronomy 4:19.

<u>God is Great</u>, Deuteronomy 4:32 – 40
Or hath God assayed to go and take him a nation from the midst of another nation, by temptations, by signs, and by wonders, and by war, and by a mighty hand, and by a

stretched out arm, and by great terrors, according to all that the LORD your God did for you in Egypt before your eyes? Deuteronomy 4:34.

Exhortation to Keep the God's Covenant, Deuteronomy 6:1 – 9
And thou shalt bind them for a sign upon thine hand, and they shall be as frontlets between thine eyes, Deuteronomy 6:8.

Remember the Past, Deuteronomy 6:20 – 25
And the LORD shewed signs and wonders, great and sore, upon Egypt, upon Pharaoh, and upon all his household, before our eyes, Deuteronomy 6:22.

The LORD will Fight for You, Deuteronomy 7:16 – 26
The great temptations which thine eyes saw, and the signs, and the wonders, and the mighty hand, and the stretched out arm, whereby the LORD thy God brought thee out: so shall the LORD thy God do unto all the people of whom thou art afraid, Deuteronomy 7:19.

The Golden Calf, Deuteronomy 9:7 – 24
And I took the 2 tables, and cast them out of my 2 hands, and brake them before your eyes, Deuteronomy 9:17.

What God Ask of Israel, Deuteronomy 10:12 – 22
He is thy praise, and he is thy God, that hath done for thee these great and terrible things, which thine eyes have seen, Deuteronomy 10:21.

Remember, Deuteronomy 11:1 – 25
But your eyes have seen all the great act of the LORD which he did, Deuteronomy 11:7.

A land which the LORD thy God careth for: the eyes of the LORD thy God are always upon it, from the beginning of the year even unto the end of the year, Deuteronomy 11:12.

Therefore, shall ye lay up these my words in your heart and in your soul, and bind them for a sign upon your hand, that they may be as frontlets between your eyes, Deuteronomy 11:18.

Place of Worship, Deuteronomy 12:1 – 14
Ye shall not do after the things that we do here this day, every man whatsoever is right in his own eyes, Deuteronomy 12:8.

A Warning Against Worshiping Other Gods,
Deuteronomy 13:12 – 18
When thou shalt hearken to the voice of the LORD thy God, to keep all his commandments which I command thee this day, to do that which is right in the eyes of the LORD thy God, Deuteronomy 13:18.

Devotion to the Lord, Deuteronomy 14:1 – 29
Ye are the children of the LORD your God: ye shall not cut yourselves, nor make any baldness between your eyes for the dead, Deuteronomy 14:1.

Justice, Deuteronomy 16:18 – 20
Thou shalt not wrest judgment; thou shall not respect persons, neither take a gift: for a gift doth blind the eyes of the wise, and pervert the words of the righteous, Deuteronomy 16:19.

Procedures Concerning Unsolved Murders,
Deuteronomy 21:1 – 9
And they shall answer and say, Our hands have not shed this blood, neither have our eyes seen it, Deuteronomy 21:7.

Laws Concerning Marriage and Divorce,
Deuteronomy 24:1 – 5
When a man hath taken a wife, and married her, and it come to pass that she find no favour in his eyes, because he hath found some uncleanness in her: then let him write her a bill of divorcement, and give it in her hand, and send her out of his house, Deuteronomy 24:1.

Israel's Consequences for Disobedience,
Deuteronomy 28:15 – 68
Thine ox shall be slain before thine eyes, and thou shalt not eat thereof: thine ass shall be violently taken away from before thy face, and shall not be restored to thee: thy sheep shall be given unto thine enemies, and thou shalt have none to rescue them, Deuteronomy 28:31.

Thy sons and thy daughters shall be given unto another people, and thine eyes shall look, and fail with longing for them all the day long; and there shall be no might in thine hand, Deuteronomy 28:32.

So that thou shalt be mad for the sight of thine eyes which thou shalt see, Deuteronomy 28:34.

And among these nations shalt thou find no ease, neither shall the sole of thy foot have rest: but the LORD shall give thee there a trembling heart, and failing of eyes, and sorrow of mind, Deuteronomy 28:65.

In the morning thou shalt say, Would God it were even! And at even thou shalt say, Would God it were morning! for the fear of thine heart wherewith thou shalt fear, and for the sight of thine eyes which thou shalt see, Deuteronomy 28:67.

Moses Reviews the Covenant, Deuteronomy 29:1 – 29
And Moses called unto all Israel, and said unto them, Ye have seen all that the LORD did before your eyes in the land of Egypt unto Pharaoh, and unto all his servants, and unto all his land, Deuteronomy 29:2.

The great temptations which thine eyes have seen, the signs, and those great miracles, Deuteronomy 29:3.

Yet the LORD hath not given you an heart to perceive, and eyes to see, and ears to hear, unto this day, Deuteronomy 29:4.

Moses at Mount Nebo, Deuteronomy 34:1 – 12
And the Lord said unto him, This is the land which I sware unto Abraham, unto Isaac, and unto Jacob, saying I will give it unto thy seed: I have caused thee to see it with thine eyes, but thou shalt not go over thither, Deuteronomy 34:4.

The word "eyes" is mentioned the most in chapter 28 of Deuteronomy. There are 68 verses in this chapter, and the word "eyes" are mentioned in 5 verses. In Deuteronomy 28, Moses is speaking to Israel. He talks to them about the blessing they will receive from God for being obedience, and curses that will come upon them for being disobedience to the laws and teachings of God.

CHAPTER 5

JOSHUA, JUDGES & RUTH

The Book of Joshua is considered by many scholars, as the first Historical Book of the Bible. The Historical Books cover approximately 1,000 years of Israel's history. These books describe and record the events of Israel from the conquest of Canaan to the Babylonian exile. The rise and fall of the northern and southern kingdoms, and the returning and rebuilding of Jerusalem.

The twelve Historical Books in the Old Testament are Joshua, Judges, Ruth, 1st Samuel, 2nd Samuel, 1st Kings, 2nd Kings, 1 Chronicles, 2nd Chronicles, Ezra, Nehemiah, and Esther.

The Book of Joshua was written between 1400 and 1370 BC. The Book of Joshua describes the Israelites entry into the land of Canaan, and the series of battles that took place among other nations which were the Hittites, Girgashites, Amorites, Canaanites, Perizzites, Hivites and Jebusites, Deuteronomy 7:1 - 3. Joshua defeated 7 kings in at least 13 battles that are described during the conquest in Canaan. Jericho was the 1st battle fought in Canaan.

The Book of Joshua tells how the territory was later divided among the twelve tribes of Israel. According to Joshua 14, it took approximately 6 years for the Israelites to conquer the Land of Canaan. The word "eyes" are mentioned in 3 verses in the Book of Joshua, which has 24 chapters.

The Lord's Commander and Joshua, Joshua 5:13 – 15
And when Josue was in the field of the city of Jericho, he lifted up his eyes, and saw a man standing over against him: holding a drawn sword, and he went to him, and said: Art thou one of ours, or of our adversaries, Joshua 5:13 DRA?

Note of Interests: Joshua was the attendant and helper of Moses during the Israelites 40 years wandering in the Sinai wilderness. He was later appointed by God to lead the Israelites after the death of Moses. Joshua led the Israelites into the Promised Land; Canaan. He is most remembered for his leadership in the marching around the wall of Jericho, which led to the destruction of the city Jericho, Joshua 6. Out of the 5 public domain Bibles; the Douay-Rheims 1899 American Edition (DRA) spells "Joshua" name "Josue."

Joshua's Final Words to Israel, Joshua 23:1 – 16
Know ye for a certainty that the LORD your God will not destroy them before your face, but they shall be a pit and a snare in your way, and a stumbling block at your side, and stakes in your eyes, till he take you away and destroy you from off this excellent land, which he hath given you, Joshua 23:13 DRA.

Note of Interests: Other men in the Bible that gave final words, which are also known as "farewell speeches" are Jacob, Genesis 49:1 – 33; Joseph, Genesis 50:24 – 26; Moses, Deuteronomy 31:1 – 8; Joshua, Joshua 24:22 – 28; David, 1 Chronicles 29:10 – 20; Jesus, Matthew 28:18 – 20; Paul, Acts 20:18 – 35.

The Lord's Covenant Renewed at Shechem, Joshua 24:1 – 28
And the children of Israel cried to the LORD: and he put
darkness between you and the Egyptians, and brought the
sea upon them, and covered them. Your eyes saw all that I
did in Egypt, and you dwelt in the wilderness a long time,
Joshua 24:7 DRA.

The Book of Judges is the 7th book in the Old Testament, and
it has 21 chapters. It covers the time between the conquest
describes in the Book of Joshua up to the establishment of
a kingdom, and the appointment of Israel's first king, Saul.

Most scholars believe that the Prophet Samuel wrote the
Book of Judges, and it was written around 1086 – 1004 BC,
during which times judges served as leaders of the people.
The 12 Judges over Israel mentioned in the Book of Judges
were Othniel, Ehud, Shamgar, Deborah, Gideon, Tola,
Jair, Jephthah, Ibzan, Elon, Abdon, and Samson. The word
"eyes" is mentioned 5 times in the Book of Judges, and they
are listed below.

Samson Betrayed by Delilah, Judges 16:1 – 22
And the Philistines seized him, and put out his eyes, and
brought him down to Gazah, and bound him with fetters
of bronze; and he had to grind in the prison-house, Judges
16:21 Darby.

Note of Interests: Delilah didn't shave off the 7 braids of
Samson's hair; she orders a servant to do it, Judges 16:18 –
21. In brief, Delilah is admired for her beauty by Samson, a
Nazirite, who possesses enormous strength. Scholars believe
his strength is equal to 10 strong, healthy men. Delilah,
a Philistine's prostitute, is paid by the five lords of the

Philistines to discover the source of Samson's strength. After 3 failed attempts by Delilah to find out Samson strength, she finally persuaded Samson to tell her; his physical strength comes from his hair.

<u>The Death of Samson</u>, Judges 16:23 – 31
And Samson called to Jehovah, and said, LORD Jehovah, remember me, I pray thee, and strengthen me, I pray thee, only this once, O God, that I may take one vengeance upon the Philistines for my two eyes, Judges 16:28 Darby.

<u>Micah's Idols and Hired Levite Priest</u>, Judges 17:1 – 13
In those days there was no king in Israel; every man did what was right in his own eyes, Judges 17:6 Darby.

<u>A Levite and His Concubine</u>, Judges 19:1 – 30
And he lifted up his eyes, and saw the wayfaring man in the open place of the city; and the old man said, Whither goest thou? And when comest thou? Judges 19:17 Darby.

Note of Interests: In biblical respect, a concubine in the Bible is considered a wife, of secondary rank. By others, the term "concubine" refers to a "female slave" or "slave wife" or "maiden." Other describes a "concubine" as a woman who lives with a man as if she were a wife, but not having the same status.

However, concubines are accepted as part of Israel's culture. Concubines were generally taken by tribal chiefs, kings, and other wealthy men. Some concubines were used to bear a male heir in the case of a barren wife. They lived in the household and was taken care of, like the 1ˢᵗ wife.

There are many men in the Bible, which had more than one concubine to provide more children to increase the family workforce and to satisfy the man's sexual desires. Abraham, Nahor, Gideon, and Saul all had concubines. King David had at least 8 wives and 10 concubines. His son, King Solomon, had about 300 concubines and 700 royal wives. Deuteronomy 17:17, forbid kings to take so many wives.

Israel Had No King, Judges 21:1 – 25
In those days there was no king in Israel; every man did what was right in his own eyes, Judges 21:25 Darby.

Note of Interests: Judges 17:1 – 13 and Judges 21:1 – 25 reads the same.

The Book of Ruth describes a biblical event of life, love, and loyalty in 4 short chapters. It was written around 1010 BC. It is a story of a Moabite woman who forsakes her pagan heritage and clings to Naomi, her mother-in-law.

Naomi's husband was named Elimelech who died and left her with two sons named Mahlon and Kilion. They were from Bethlehem in Judah, who had moved to Moab to live because of the famine in Judah. They lived in Moab for about 10 years, and the sons had married Moabite women, one was named Orpah, and the other was named Ruth. Naomi's sons also died, and they had no children by their wives.

Soon afterward, Naomi told her 2 daughters-in-law to return to their father's household so they could have a better life. However, Ruth refused to go back, but Orpah did. Ruth remained with Naomi and cared for her on her journey back to her hometown.

Once Naomi and Ruth return to Judah, Ruth begins to glean in barley fields for food each day, for her and Naomi. Ruth runs into a wealthy landowner named Boaz. He instantly takes a liking to her. He offers her all kinds of gleaning privileges because he heard about her and her mother-in-law.

Boaz is also a close relative of Naomi's deceased husband, Elimelech. According to Jewish law, Boaz had the right to marry Ruth after the death of her husband. Naomi encourages Ruth to go to Boaz in the evening and present herself willing to accept a marriage proposal from him. Boaz was pleased, but there was one relative who was closer in line to marry Ruth.

The next day, Boaz met with this relative and presented his case. The relative turned down the offer to marry Ruth. Then Boaz makes a commitment in front of the town's leaders that he would take Ruth as his wife.

God's providence and the kinsman redeemer are 2 of the main themes in the Book of Ruth. The key individuals in this book are Naomi, Ruth, and Boaz. The name Naomi means "pleasant." Ruth name means "friend," and Boaz name means "he comes in strength." Boaz brings a Moabite woman into the family line of David, and eventually of Christ. The name of Ruth and Boaz son is "Obed," which means "servant." The word "eyes" are mentioned twice in chapter 2 of Ruth.

Ruth Meets Boaz, Ruth 2:1 – 23
Let thine eyes be on the field that they do reap, and go thou after them: have I not charged the young men that they shall not touch thee? And when thou art athirst, go unto the vessels, and drink of that which the young men have drawn, Ruth 2:9 ASV.

Then she fell on her face, and bowed herself to the ground, and said unto him, Why have I found favour in thine eyes, that thou shouldest regard me, seeing I am a foreigner, Ruth 2:10 Darby?

CHAPTER 6

THE BOOKS OF 1ST AND 2ND SAMUEL

The books of 1st and 2nd Samuel are 2 of the historical books in the KJV Old Testament. They were originally a single book and still are in the Hebrew Bible. They are named after the Prophet Samuel. The books of 1st and 2nd Samuel covers the life of Samuel, as well as the first two kings of Israel; Saul and David.

The Prophet Samuel is 1st mentioned in the Bible as a baby, 1 Samuel 1:20. His parents were Elkanah and Hannah. His mother Hannah was barren, but God heard her prayer and opened her womb, blessing her with the baby Samuel. After Samuel was weaned from his mother, his parents dedicated him to the LORD, and place him under the care of Eli, the priest. Samuel was trained and raised in the temple.

Note of Interests: Samuel's birth is an answered prayer by his mother. She was praying and pleading to God at the tabernacle in Shiloh. She asked God to allow her to bear a son. Hannah promised God that if He let her bear a son, she would give him to the service of God, 1 Samuel 1:11. Samuel is considered a miracle child, along with Isaac, Samson, John the Baptist, Jacob/Esau, Perez and his brother, Zerah.

Samuel name means "God has heard." Samuel is from the tribe of Levi and considered the last judge. After Joshua died, Israel enters the "days of the judges, and there was no centralized government. During this time, God raises up individuals to deliver Israel from her enemies, Judges 2:16.

The Book of Judges speak on 12 judges that ruled over Israel, and the Book of 1st Samuel mentions two more judges named Eli and Samuel. After Samuel served as judge over Israel, Israel is granted kings to rule over them. Israel had judges for about 450 years, then Israel request a king, and God gave them one, Acts 13:20.

The Prophet Samuel anointed the first 2 kings of Israel who were Saul and David. When the people of Israel demanded a king, God directed Samuel to anoint Saul, who was from the tribe of Benjamin. When Saul started disobeying God, God has Samuel to anoint a young shepherd named David, as the new future king.

The Prophet Samuel begins his ministry serving the chief priest in the tabernacle, 1 Samuel 3:1. Samuel made sacrifices on behalf of the people of Israel and offered intercessory prayers to God for them, 1 Samuel 7:9. Samuel was a Nazarite, like the mighty Samson.

Note of Interests: Samuel is the only ghost in the Bible. He was summoned from the grave, then he rose from the ground in a spirit form wearing a robe, and spoke to Saul, 1 Samuel 28:3 – 14.

After Samuel dies, Saul meets with the witch of Endor, 1 Samuel 28:7. The witch conjures up the spirit of Samuel, who isn't pleased about Saul disturbing him, 1 Samuel 28:15 – 19.

The Prophet Samuel is noted for having the greatest Passover. Hundreds of years after Samuel's death, a king name Josiah in his 18th year as king, celebrated the Passover in a grand and awe-inspiring way. The writer of 2 Chronicles says, "it's the greatest Passover ever, since Samuel's day," 2 Chronicles 35:18.

Question: Who was King Josiah? I just couldn't resist asking. *Smile*

Answer in the back of the book

The Prophet Samuel is also remembered for being a praying man in the 99th Psalms, which has only 9 verses. Samuel is compared with Moses and Aaron, as one who called upon the Lord's name, Psalm 99:6. Samuel was one of a few men in the Bible that were extremely obedient to God.

Note of Interests: The LORD called Samuel by name 4 times, but on the 4th call, the LORD called Samuel's name twice, "Samuel Samuel!," 1 Samuel 3:10. Samuel is one of 7 people in the Bible that the LORD called their names back-to- back in the same sentence; twice. The others are Abraham (Genesis 22:11), Jacob (Genesis 46:2), Moses (Exodus 3:4), Martha (Luke 10:41), Saul (Acts 9:4), and Simon (Luke 22:31).

PS: The event surrounding why the LORD called their names twice is in the back of the book. God Bless.

First Samuel has 31 chapters, and 2nd Samuel has 24 chapters. In 1st Samuel, the word "eyes" are mentioned 17 times in 16 verses; twice in 1 Samuel 26:24. Those verses are listed below in the King James Version with a subject title.

The Prophecy Against Eli's Family, 1 Samuel 2:22 – 36
And the man of thine, whom I shall not cut off from mine altar, shall be to consume thine eyes, and to grieve thine heart: and all the increase of thine house shall die in the flower of their age, 1 Samuel 2:33.

The Lord Calls to Samuel, 1 Samuel 3:1 – 18
And it came to pass at that time, when Eli was laid down in his place, and his eyes began to wax dim, that he could not see, 1 Samuel 3:2.

The Death of Eli, 1 Samuel 4:1 – 22
Now Eli was 98 years old; and his eyes were dim, that he could not see, 1 Samuel 4:15.

The Return of the Ark to Israel, 1 Samuel 6:1 – 21
And they of Bethshemesh were reaping their wheat harvest in the valley: and they lifted up their eyes, and saw the ark, and rejoiced to see it, 1 Samuel 6:13.

Saul Defeats the Ammonites, 1 Samuel 11:1 - 15
And Nahash the Ammonite answered them, On this condition will I make a covenant with you, that I may thrust out all your eyes, and lay it for a reproach upon all Israel, 1 Samuel 11:2.

Samuel's Farewell Speech to the People, 1 Samuel 12:1 – 25

Behold, here I am: witness against me before the LORD, and before his anointed: whose ox have I taken? Or whose ass have I taken? Or whom have I defrauded? Whom have I oppressed? Or of whose hand have I received any bribe to blind mine eyes therewith? And I will restore it you, 1 Samuel 12:3.

Now therefore stand and see this great thing, which the LORD will do before your eyes, 1 Samuel 12:16.

<u>Saul Make Another Mistake with an Oath</u>, 1 Samuel 14:24 – 46
But Jonathan heard not when his father charged the people with the oath: wherefore he put forth the end of the rod that was in his hand, and dipped it in an honeycomb, and put his hand to his mouth; and his eyes were enlightened, 1 Samuel 14:27.

Then said Jonathan, My father hath troubled the land: see, I pray you, how mine eyes have been enlightened, because I tasted a little of this honey, 1 Samuel 14:29.

<u>Jonathan and David's Covenant</u>, 1 Samuel 20:1 – 42
And David sware moreover, and said, Thy father certainly knoweth that I found grace in thine eyes; and he saith, Let not Jonathan know this, lest he be grieved: but truly as the LORD liveth, and as thy soul liveth, there is but a step between me and death, 1 Samuel 20:3.

And he said, Let me go, I pray thee; for our family hath a sacrifice in the city; and by brother, he hath commanded me to be there: and now, if I have found favour in thine eyes, let me get away, I pray thee, and see my brethren. Therefore, he cometh not unto the king's table, 1 Samuel 20:29.

David Spares Saul's Life, 1 Samuel 24:1 – 22
Behold, this day thine eyes have seen how that the LORD
had delivered thee to day into mine hand in the cave: and
some bade me kill thee: but mine eye spared thee; and I said,
I will not put forth mine hand against my lord; for the is the
LORD's anointed, 1 Samuel 24:10.

David, Nabal and Abigail, 1 Samuel 25:1 – 44
Ask thy young men, and they will shew thee. Wherefore
let the young men find favour in thine eyes: for we come in
a good day: give, I pray thee, whatsoever cometh to thine
hand unto thy servants, and to thy son David, 1 Samuel 25:8.

David Spares Saul's Life Again, 1 Samuel 26:1 – 25
Then said Saul, I have sinned: return, my son David: for I
will no more do thee harm, because my soul was precious in
thine eyes this day: behold, I have played the fool, and have
erred exceedingly, 1 Samuel 26:21.

And, behold, as thy life was much set by this day in mine
eyes, so let my life be much set by in the eyes of the LORD,
and let him deliver me out of all tribulation, 1 Samuel 26:24.

David Flees to the Philistines, 1 Samuel 27:1 – 12
And David said unto Achish, If I have now found grace in
thine eyes, let them give me a place in some town in the
country, that I may dwell there: for why should thy servant
dwell in the royal city with thee, 1 Samuel 27:5?

The 10th book of the KJV Old Testament is 2nd Samuel.
Second Samuel opens with the death of King Saul. It
describes David's rise to power, first at Hebron in Judah,
and then at Jerusalem over all Israel. The word "eyes"

is mentioned in 8 verses, which are recorded from the American Standard Version (ASV).

King David Leaping and Jumping, 2 Samuel 6:12 – 23
Then David returned to bless his household. And Michal the daughter of Saul came out to meet David, and said, How glorious was the king of Israel to-day, who uncovered himself to-day in the eyes of the handmaids of his servants, as one of the vain fellows shamelessly uncovereth himself, 2 Samuel 6:20!

Nathaniel's Parable to David, 2 Samuel 12:1 – 15
Thus saith Jehovah, Behold, I will raise up evil against thee out of thine own house; and I will take thy wives before thine eyes, and give them unto thy neighbour, and he shall lie with thy wives in the sight of this sun, 2 Samuel 12:11.

Absalom Flees to Geshur, 2 Samuel 13:1 – 39
But Absalom fled. And the young man that kept the watch lifted up his eyes, and looked, and, behold, there came much people by the way of the hill-side behind him, 2 Samuel 13:34.

David and His People Escape, 2 Samuel 15:13 – 37
And the king said unto Zadok, Carry back the ark of God into the city: if I shall find favor in the eyes of the Jehovah, he will bring me again, and show me both it, and his habitation, 2 Samuel 15:25.

Absalom's Army Defeated, 2 Samuel 18:6 – 33
Now David was sitting between the two gates: and the watchmen went up to the roof of the gate unto the wall, and lifted up his eyes, and looked, and behold a man running alone, 2 Samuel 18:24.

David Shows Kindness to Mephibosheth,
2 Samuel 19:24 – 30
And he hath slandered thy servant unto my lord the king; but my lord the king is as an angel of God: do therefore what is good in thine eyes, 2 Samuel 19:27.

David's Song of Praise to the LORD, 2 Samuel 22:1 – 51
And the afflicted people thou wilt save; But thine eyes are upon the haughty, that thou mayest bring them down, 2 Samuel 22:28.

Joab Counts the Fighting Men, 2 Samuel 24:1 – 9
And Joab said unto the king, Now the Jehovah thy God add unto the people, how many soever they may be, an hundredfold; and may the eyes of my lord the king see it: but why doth my lord the king delight in this thing, 2 Samuel 24:3?

CHAPTER 7

THE BOOKS OF 1ST
AND 2ND KINGS

The books of 1st and 2nd Kings were once one book, along with 1st and 2nd Samuel, and 1st and 2nd Chronicles. The Book of 1st Kings begins with the elderly King David, who was advanced in years and couldn't keep warm. His servants sought a young virgin woman to attend to King David. They found Abishag, a Shunammite to care for and serve the king, but the king did not have sexual relations with her, 1 Kings 1:4.

The Book of 1st Kings records King David's son named Adonijah. He tried to seize the throne, before King David officially turns the Kingdom of Israel over to his son, Solomon. Adonijah was the 4th son of David, and his mother was Haggith.

The Book of 1st Kings also describes the rule of Solomon as the last king of Israel. After the death of Solomon, his son Rehoboam begin to reign, and then the split of the kingdom occurred. The 12 tribes were divided, and the southern part of the land was called the Kingdom of Judah, which consist of 2 tribes; Judah and Benjamin. The northern part of the land was called the Kingdom of Israel, which consist of 10 tribes; Reuben, Simeon, Manasseh, Issachar, Zebulun, Ephraim, Dan, Asher, Naphtali, and Gad.

Jeroboam became the 1st king of the northern kingdom of Israel. Before Jeroboam received a prophecy concerning becoming king by Prophet Ahijah, he was a skilled worker for King Solomon. Later Solomon placed Jeroboam over the labor force of the tribes of Joseph, 1 Kings 11:28. The Prophet Ahijah prophesied that upon Solomon's death, Jeroboam would become king over 10 tribes.

The Book of 1st Kings speaks on the kings, who obey and disobey God during the ruling of the kings of Israel and Judah. The Book of 1st Kings was written about 560 BC. The main individual mentioned in 1st Kings are David, Solomon, Rehoboam, Jeroboam, Elijah, Ahab and Jezebel.

The Book of 2nd Kings is narrative history concerning the affairs of the divided kingdoms. It was written around 560 – 538 B.C. The main prophets mentioned in 2nd Kings are Elijah and Elisha. Other individuals mentioned in 2nd Kings are the woman who lived in Shunem, Naaman, Jezebel, Jehu, Joash, Hezekiah, Sennacherib, Isaiah, Manasseh, Josiah, Jehoiakim, Zedekiah, and Nebuchadnezzar.

The Book of 1st Kings have 22 chapters, and 2nd Kings have 25 chapters. The word "eyes" is mentioned in a total of 26 verses in 1st and 2nd Kings. They are listed below with an inspirational subject title.

P.S. I pray in Jesus' name, the subject title tugs at your heart, mind, soul, and spirit to encourage you to read the verses that surround the word "eyes." Be Bless!

The Book of 1st Kings

Nathan and Bathsheba Speaks to David, 1 Kings 1:11 – 27 And thou, my lord, O king, the eyes of all Israel are upon thee, that thou shouldest tell them who shall sit on the throne of my lord the king after him, 1 Kings 1:20.

<u>King David Anointed Solomon King</u>, 1 Kings 1:28 – 53
And also thus said the king, Blessed be the LORD God of Israel, which hath given one to sit on my throne this day, mine eyes even seeing it, 1 Kings 1:48.

<u>Solomon's Prays at the Temple</u>, 1 Kings 8: 22 – 61
That thine eyes may be open toward this house night and day, even toward the place of which thou hast said, My name shall be there: that thou mayest hearken unto the prayer which thy servant shall make toward this place, 1 Kings 8:29.

That thine eyes may be open unto the supplication of thy servant, and unto the supplication of thy people Israel to hearken unto them in all that they call for unto thee, 1 Kings 8:52.

<u>The LORD Hears Solomon's Prayer</u>, 1 Kings 9:1 – 9
And the LORD said unto him, I have heard thy prayer and thy supplication, that thou hast made before me: I have hallowed this house, which thou hast built, to put my name there for ever; and mine eyes and mine heart shall be there perpetually, 1 Kings 9:3.

<u>The Queen of Sheba Visits Solomon</u>, 1 Kings 10:1 – 13
Howbeit I believed not the words, until I came, and mine eyes had seen it: and behold, the half was not told me: thy wisdom and prosperity exceedeth the fame which I heard, 1 Kings 10:7.

<u>The LORD Promise to Jeroboam</u>, 1 Kings 11:26 – 40
Because that they have forsaken me, and have worshipped Ashtoreth the goddess of the Zidonians, Chemosh the god of the Moabites, and Milcom the god of the children of Ammon, and have not walked in my ways, to do that

which is right in mine eyes, and to keep my statues and my judgments, as did David his father, 1 Kings 11:33.

Jeroboam's Son, Abijah Dies, 1 Kings 14:1 – 18
And Jeroboam's wife did so, and arose, and went to Shiloh, and came to the house of Ahijah. But Ahijah could not see; for his eyes were set by reasons of his age, 1 Kings 14:4.

And rent the kingdom away from the house of David and gave it thee: and yet thou hast not been as my servant David, who kept my commandments, and who followed me with all his heart, to do that only which was right in mine eyes, 1 Kings 14:8.

Abijam Reigns in Judah, 1 Kings 15:1 – 8
Because David did that which was right in the eyes of the LORD, and turned not aside from any thing that he commanded him all the days of his life, save only in the matter or Uriah the Hittite, 1 Kings 15:5.

Asa Reigns in Judah, 1 Kings 15:9 – 24
And Asa did that which was right in the eyes of the LORD, as did David his father, 1 Kings 15:11.

Omri Reigns in Israel, 1 Kings 16:21 – 28
But Omri wrought evil in the eyes of the LORD and did worse than all that were before him, 1 Kings 16:25.

Ben-Hadad Attacks Samaria, 1 Kings 20:1 – 12
Yet I will send my servants unto thee to morrow about this time, and they shall search thine house, and the houses of thy servants; and it shall be, that whatsoever is pleasant in

thine eyes, they shall put it in their hand, and take it away, 1 Kings 20:6.

Jehoshaphat Reigns in Judah, 1 Kings 22:41 – 50
And Jehoshaphat walked in all the ways of Asa his father; he turned not aside from it, doing that which was right in the eyes of the LORD: nevertheless the high places were not taken away; for the people offered and burnt incense yet in the high places, 1 Kings 22:43.

The Book of 2nd Kings

Elisha and the Shunammite Woman, 2 Kings 4:8 – 37
And he went up, and lay upon the child, and put his mouth upon his mouth, and his eyes upon his eyes, and his hands upon his hands: and stretched himself upon the child; and the flesh of the child waxed warm, 2 Kings 4:34.

Then he returned and walked in the house to and fro; and went up and stretched himself upon him: and the child sneezed 7 times, and the child opened his eyes, 2 Kings 4:35.

Horses and Chariots of Fire Surrounds Elisha, 2 Kings 6:8 – 23
And Elisha prayed, and said, LORD, I pray thee, open his eyes, that he may see. And the LORD opened the eyes of the young man; and he saw: and behold, the mountain was full of horses and chariots of fire round about Elisha, 2 Kings 6:17.

And it came to pass, when they were come into Samaria, that Elisha said, LORD, open the eyes of these men, that they may see. And the LORD opened their eyes, and they saw; and, behold, they were in the midst of Samaria, 2 Kings 6:20.

Elisha Predicts Deliverance, 2 Kings 7:1 – 20
Then a lord on whose hand the king leaned answered the man of God, and said, Behold, if the LORD would make windows in heaven, might this thing be? And he said, Behold, thou shalt see it with thine eyes, but shalt not eat thereof, 2 Kings 7:2.

And that lord answered the man of God, and said, Now, behold, if the LORD should make windows in heaven, might such a thing be? And he said, Behold, thou shalt see it with thine eyes, but shalt not eat thereof, 2 Kings 7:19.

Jehu Put to Death All of Ahab's Descendants, 2 Kings 10:1 – 17
And he that was over the house, and he that was over the city, the elders also, and the bringers up of the children, sent to Jehu, saying, We are thy servants, and will do all that thou shalt bid us; we will not make any king: do thou that which is good in thine eyes, 2 Kings 10:5.

Jehu Executes Baal Worshipers, 2 Kings 10:18 – 33
And the LORD said unto Jehu, Because thou hast done well in executing that which is right in mine eyes, and hast done unto the house of Ahab according to all that was in mine heart, thy children of the 4th generation shall sit on the throne of Israel, 2 Kings 10:30.

King Hezekiah's Prayer, 2 Kings 19:14 – 19
LORD, bow down thine ear, and hear: open, LORD, thine eyes, and see: and hear the words of Sennacherib, which hath sent him to reproach the living God, 2 Kings 9:16.

Isaiah Predicts King Hezekiah Victory over Sennacherib,
2 Kings 19:20 – 34
Whom hast thou reproached and blasphemed? And against
whom hast thou exalted thy voice, and lifted up thine eyes
on high? Even against the Holy One of Israel, 2 Kings 19:22.

Hilkiah the High Priest Discovers God's Law,
2 Kings 22:8 – 20
Behold, therefore, I will gather thee unto thy fathers, and
thou shalt be gathered into thy grave in peace; and thine eyes
shall not see all the evil which I will bring upon this place.
And they brought the king word again, 2 Kings 22:20.

The Fall of Jerusalem, 2 Kings 25:1 – 7
And they slew the sons of Zedekiah before his eyes and
put out the eyes of Zedekiah and bound him with fetters of
brass, and carried him to Babylon, 2 Kings 25:7.

CHAPTER 8

THE BOOKS OF 1ST AND 2ND CHRONICLES

A chronicle is a historical account of information, facts, and detail events arranged in chronological orders; organized in the order of occurrence. The Greek word "chronos" means "time," and the word "chronicles" is related to "chronological" and comes from the Greek word "ta khronika," which means "annals of time."

The books of 1ˢᵗ and 2ⁿᵈ Chronicles retells the life events of the Israelites. Jewish traditions state that Ezra wrote 1ˢᵗ and 2ⁿᵈ Chronicles. However, many scholars refer to the author of Chronicles as anonymous.

The books of 1ˢᵗ and 2ⁿᵈ Chronicles were originally one book that summarizes the history and genealogies of the Israelites up to the reign of King David. These books focus on the reigns of David, Solomon, and the kings of Judea. The books of 1ˢᵗ and 2ⁿᵈ Chronicles can be outlined as follow.

1. Genealogies from Adam to David, 1 Chronicles 1 – 9
2. David Rules a United Israel, 1 Chronicles 10 – 29
3. Solomon Builds the Temple, 2 Chronicles 1 – 9
4. From Jerusalem to Babylonian Captivity, 2 Chronicles 10 – 36

The books of 1ˢᵗ and 2ⁿᵈ Chronicles is full of genealogies. God's covenant with David is mentioned, and the events that surround the covenant. Chronicles focus on God's covenant with David and the temple. David planned the temple, Solomon builds it, many kings were crowned in it, some prophets were killed in it, and the law was rediscovered in it.

The first 9 chapters of 1st Chronicles cover the time that took place from Genesis 2 to 1st Samuel which is from Adam to David. It traces David's ancestry along with the other major families in the 12 tribes of Israel.

When David reign, he was a good king who followed God. He united the tribes of Israel and delivered them from their enemies. God makes an everlasting covenant with David. He told David that Solomon's throne would be established forever, 1 Chronicles 17.

David draws up plans to make a magnificent temple for the LORD. Before David died, he charges Solomon and the people with building the temple and being faithful to the LORD, 1 Chronicles 28.

When Solomon reign, he asked God for wisdom instead of riches, long life, or the deaths of his adversaries. God was pleased with his request, and grants Solomon wisdom, along with riches and power. Solomon built the temple of God in Jerusalem. Israel flourishes under Solomon's reign, becoming the most prominent nation in the world, 2 Chronicles 9.

When Solomon's son Rehoboam reigned, the kingdom splits after Solomon dies. There were 10 tribes that rebel and form a new kingdom in the North. The tribes of Judah and Benjamin remain loyal to David's royal line. The kings that reigned didn't serve the LORD the way David did.

They neglect God's temple, ignored His law, persecute His prophets, and worshiped other gods. A few good kings brought about revival, but eventually, God disciplines his people for forsaking him.

The Babylonians destroyed Jerusalem, demolished the temple, and carry the children of Israel into captivity for 70 years. Afterward, the Persian king Cyrus decrees that the temple be rebuilt.

The books of Chronicles concentrate on the Southern Kingdom called Judah. The word "eyes" is mentioned in 16 verses in the books of 1st and 2nd Chronicles. In 1st Chronicles, the word "eyes" is mentioned 4 times, within 29 chapters. The word "eyes" is mentioned 12 times in 2nd Chronicles, which has 36 chapters. The verses of 1st and 2nd Chronicles listed below are recorded from the World English Bible, (WEB).

The Book of 1 Chronicles

Bringing Back the Ark from Kiriath Jearim,
1 Chronicles 13:1 – 14
All the assembly said that they would do so; for the thing was right in the eyes of all the people, 1 Chronicles 13:4.

God's Promise to David, 1 Chronicles 17:1 – 15
This was a small thing in your eyes, God; but you have spoken of your servant's house for a great while to come, and have respected me according to the standard of a man of high degree, Yahweh God, 1 Chronicles 17.17.

<u>David Sins by Counting Israel</u>, 1 Chronicles 21:1 – 17
David lifted up his eyes, and saw Yahweh's angel standing between the earth and the sky, having a drawn sword in his hand stretched out over Jerusalem. Then David and the elders, clothed in sackcloth, fell on their faces, 1 Chronicles 21:16.

<u>David Buys Araunah's Threshing Floor</u>, 1 Chronicles 21:18 – 30
Ornan said to David, "Take it for yourself, and let my lord the king do that which is good in his eyes. Behold, I give the oxen for burnt offerings, and the threshing instruments for wood, and the wheat for the meat offering. I give it all," 1 Chronicles 21:23.

The 2 Book of Chronicles opens with Solomon ruling as king over Israel and ends with Persian King Cyrus speaking to the exiled Jews in Babylonia.

Thus saith Cyrus king of Persia,
All the kingdoms of the earth hath Jehovah,
the God of heaven, given me;
and he hath charged me to build him a house
in Jerusalem, which is in Judah. Whosoever
there is among you of all his people,
Jehovah his God be with him, and let him go up.
2 Chronicles 36:23 ASV

<u>Solomon Pray at the Temple</u>, 2 Chronicles 6:12 – 42
That thine eyes may be open upon this house day and night, upon the place whereof thou hast said that thou wouldest put thy name there; to hearken unto the prayer which thy servant prayeth toward this place, 2 Chronicles 6:20.

Now, my God, let, I beseech thee, thine eyes be open, and let thine ears be attent unto the prayer that is made in this place, 2 Chronicles 6:40.

The LORD Appears to Solomon, 2 Chronicles 7:11 – 22
Now mine eyes shall be open, and mine ears attent unto the prayer that is made in this place, 2 Chronicles 7:15.

For now have I chosen and sanctified this house, that my name may be there for ever: and mine eyes and mine heart shall be there perpetually, 2 Chronicles 7:16.

The Queen of Sheba Visits Solomon, 2 Chronicles 9:1 - 12
Howbeit I believed not their words, until I came, and mine eyes had seen it: and, behold, the one half of the greatness of thy wisdom was not told me: for thou exceedest the fame that I head, 2 Chronicles 9:6.

Asa Reigns in Judah, 2 Chronicles 14:1 – 15
And Asa did that which was good and right in the eyes of the LORD his God, 2 Chronicles 14:2.

Hanani the Prophet Condemns Asa, 2 Chronicles 16:7 – 10
For the eyes of the LOR run to and fro throughout the whole earth, to shew himself strong in the behalf of the whose heart is perfect toward him. Herein thou hast done foolishly: therefore, from henceforth thou shalt have wars, 2 Chronicles 16:9.

Jehoshaphat's Victory against Moab and Ammon, 2 Chronicles 20:1 – 30
O our God, wilt thou not judge them? For we have not might against this great company that cometh against us;

neither know we what to do: but our eyes are upon thee, 2 Chronicles 20:12.

King Jehoram of Judah, 2 Chronicles 21:2 – 20
And he walked in the way of the kings of Israel, like as did the house of Ahab: for he had the daughter of Ahab to wife: and he wrought that which was evil in the eyes of the LORD, 2 Chronicles 21:6.

King Hezekiah of Judah, 2 Chronicles 29:1 – 19
For our fathers have trespassed and done that which was evil in the eyes of the LORD or God, and have forsaken him, and have turned away their faces from the habitation of the LORD, and turned their backs, 2 Chronicles 29:6.

Wherefore the wrath of the LORD was upon Judah and Jerusalem, and he hath delivered them to trouble, to astonishment, and to hissing, as ye see with your eyes, 2 Chronicles 29:8.

Prophetess Huldah's Prophecy of Judgment,
2 Chronicles 34:22 – 28
Behold, I will gather thee to thy fathers, and thou shalt be gathered to thy grave in peace, neither shall thine eyes see all the evil that I will bring upon this place, and upon the inhabitants of the same. So, they brought the king word again, 2 Chronicles 34:28.

CHAPTER 9

EZRA, NEHEMIAH & ESTHER

The books of Ezra, Nehemiah, and Esther are the last 3 historical books in the Old Testament. These books record what happened to the Jewish people after the Babylonian Captivity which lasted 70 years.

Note of Interests: The word "seventy" is mentioned 60 times in the KJV Bible. In the Old Testament, it is mentioned 57 times, and 3 times in the New Testament.

The number "70" is made up of two numbers, which are number 7 and 10. The number 7 represents "perfection," and the number 10 represents "completeness and God's law." The number "70" is also associated with "a period of judgment."

According to Exodus 1:5, a total of 70 descendants of Jacob went down to Egypt. They started the Jewish population in Egypt, which later grew to over 2 million by the time of the exodus.

According to Exodus 24:9 – 11, Moses took 70 elders of Israel along with Aaron, and his sons, Nadab and Abihu up to Mount Sinai; there they ate and drank with God. The 70 elders became known as the Sanhedrin; the Jewish court system.

According to Numbers 11:16 – 18, God told Moses to appoint 70 elders of Israel to stand with him to bear the burden of the people at the Tabernacle.

According to Jeremiah 25:11 – 12, the Israelites were exiled in Babylon 70 years.

According to Daniel 9:20 – 24, the angel Gabriel told Daniel that God had decided for 70 weeks the people would suffer for their sins, before justice rule forever.

According to Luke 10:1 – 17 (KJV), Jesus sent 70 disciples out to preach the Gospel to the surrounding area.

Ezra and Nehemiah were originally a single book; called Ezra-Nehemiah. The Book of Ezra focuses on rebuilding the temple, and the Book of Nehemiah focuses on rebuilding the city of Jerusalem. The Book of Esther focuses on events that happen in Persia when Ahasuerus, also known by his Greek name, Xerxes who was king around 465 BC.

The Book of Ezra has 10 chapters, Nehemiah has 13 chapters, and Esther has 10 chapters. The word "eyes" is mentioned in each book, twice, and they are listed below with a subject title.

The Book of Ezra

Scholars consider the Book of Ezra as the first book from the post-exilic period of Israel. The book starts where the book of 2nd Chronicles ends. The Book of Ezra begins its history at the beginning of the Medo-Persian rule, and it was written around 440 BC, shortly after Ezra returned to Jerusalem.

Cyrus, the King of Persia, had conquered the Babylonian. He put out a decree for the Jews to go back to re-inhabit Jerusalem and re-build the Temple. After the first group of Jews returned to Jerusalem, it was 78 years later, when a second group returned to the city. Zerubbabel led the first group, Ezra 1 – 6; and Ezra led the second group of people, Ezra 7 – 10. He was a priest, the son of Saraiah, a scribe, and a godly man, Ezra 7:1 - 10.

History records that King Nebuchadnezzar invaded Israel and carried the Jews away as captives around 606 BC. Israel was under Babylonian control until approximately 536 BC, when the Medo-Persians Empire took control.

The word "eyes" is mentioned in chapters 3 and 9 of Ezra.

Rebuilding the Altar and Temple, Ezra 3:1 – 13
But many of the priests and Levites and chief of the fathers, who were ancient men, that had seen the 1st house, when the foundation of this house was laid before their eyes, wept with a loud voice; and many shouted aloud for joy, Ezra 3:12 KJV.

Ezra's Prayer of Repentance, Ezra 9:5 – 15
And now for a little space there hath been favour from Jehovah our God, to leave us a remnant to escape, and to give us a nail in his holy place, that our God may lighten our eyes, and give us a little reviving in our bondage, Ezra 9:8 Darby.

The Book of Nehemiah

Nehemiah around 430 BC wrote the Book of Nehemiah, which is the 16th book of the Old Testament. It records the events surrounding the Jews return to Jerusalem, and the rebuilding of the city walls in 445 BC. Jerusalem had a temple, but there was no protection for the city.

Nehemiah means "Jehovah has comforted." He urged the people to rebuild Jerusalem's walls. He was a cupbearer to the Persian King Artaxerxes. A cupbearer was an officer of high rank in the royal courts. He was responsible for serving drinks at the royal table. On many accounts, the cupbearer tasted the wine and ate the food before the king did, to make sure no one had poisoned the king's wine or food.

When Nehemiah learned that the walls of Jerusalem were broken down, he immediately asked the king for permission to return and rebuild the city. The king granted Nehemiah request and gave him resources, and authority to accomplish the task. The word "eyes" is mentioned first in Nehemiah's prayer, chapter 1 and then Nehemiah 6.

Note of Interests: Nehemiah set up guards to defend against the constant threat of those who opposed their efforts, which included the armies of Samaria, the Ammonites, and the Ashdodites. He also ordered nobles and officials to forgive all outstanding debts. They had to return all land and money that had been taken as taxes. The repairing and rebuilding of Jerusalem's walls and gates were completed in 52 days, Nehemiah 6:15. The length of the walls was approximately 2.5 miles. The average height was about 40 feet, and the thickness of the wall was 8.2 feet. The wall of Jerusalem contained 34 watchtowers, 7 main gates, and 2 minor gates.

<u>Nehemiah's Prayer</u>, Nehemiah 1:4 – 11
Let thine ear now be attentive, and thine eyes open, to hear the prayer of thy servant, which I pray before thee at this time, day and night, for the children of Israel thy servants, confessing the sins of the children of Israel, which we have sinned against thee: both I and my father's house have sinned, Nehemiah 1:6 Darby.

<u>The Wall is Finished</u>, Nehemiah 6:15 – 19
And it came to pass that when all our enemies heard [of it], all the nations that were about us were afraid and were much cast down in their own eyes, and they perceived that this work was wrought of our God, Nehemiah 6:16 Darby.

The Book of Esther

Esther was a Jewish woman, a descendant of the tribe of Benjamin. Her ancestors were the Jews who had been carried captive to Babylon nearly 100 years earlier. Esther risked her life to save her people, the Jews.

Note of Interests: Esther was an orphan who was raised in the house of her older cousin named Mordecai, Esther 2:7. According to Esther 2:15, Abihail is the name of Esther's father, and his name means "father of might." The mother of Esther is not mentioned. In the Old Testament, there are 5 people named Abihail, 2 of them are women, and 3 are men.

The Book of Esther takes place in the Persian Empire during the reign of King Xerxes, who is also known as King Ahasuerus, the son of Darius the Great. The Book of Esther begins with King Xerxes throwing an enormous party. When he summons his wife, Queen Vashi, to come to show off her beauty, she refused. As a result, she was banned, and the king search for a new queen begins, who ends up being Esther.

Note of Interests: The king's party in the Book of Esther lasted 180-days. King Xerxes ruled over 127 provinces.

The word "eyes" is mentioned in Esther, chapters 1 and 8, only.

Queen Vashti Disobeys King Xerxes, Esther 1:1 – 22
For this deed of the queen shall come abroad unto all women, so that they shall despise their husbands in their eyes, when it shall be reported, The king Ahasuerus commanded Vashti the queen to be brought in before him, but she came not, Esther 1:17 KJV.

Esther Saves the Jews, Esther 8:1 – 17
And said, If it please the king, and if I have favour in his sight, and the thing seem right before the king, and I be pleasing in his eyes, let it be written to reverse the letters devised by Haman the son of Hammedatha the Agagite, which he wrote to destroy the Jews which are in all the king's provinces, Esther 8:5 KJV.

CHAPTER 10
THE 1ST POETIC BOOK

The Book of Job is the 1st poetic book in the Old Testament with 42 chapters. The other poetic books are Psalms, Proverbs, Ecclesiastes, and Song of Songs. These books are oftentimes called wisdom books. The Book of Job is described as the book to go to in time of affliction.

The Book of Job opens describing a man in the land of Uz. His name was Job, and he was a perfect, blameless, upright man who fears God. Job had 7 sons and 3 daughters. He was a wealthy man with 7,000 sheep, 3,000 camels, 500 yokes of oxen, 500 female donkeys, and many servants.

In the course of one day, Job lost all his possessions through various catastrophes. The first thing that happens to Job, the Sabeans attacked and killed his servants, then stole his oxen, and donkeys. Next, a servant of Job told him, the fire of God fell from heaven and burned up the sheep and his servants who were attending the sheep.

While the servant was still speaking a messenger came, he told Job that the Chaldeans and made off with his camels and put his servants to the sword. While this messenger was still speaking, another messenger came, and he told Job that his sons and daughters were feasting at the oldest brother's house. Suddenly, a mighty wind swept in and struck the 4 corners of the house. The house collapsed on them, and they were all killed.

After hearing this, Job got up, tore his robe, and shaved his head. Job fell to the ground in worship. He said in prayer, "Naked came I from my mother's womb, and naked I will return. The LORD gave, and the LORD hath taken away, may the name of the LORD be blessed." In his calamities and suffering, Job did not sin by charging God with wrongdoing.

The Book of Job speaks on the problem of human suffering and demonstrate the sovereignty of God. In the Book of Job, there is a dialogue between Job and his 3 friends named Eliphaz, Bildad, and Zophar. The Lord speech twice and the book closed with Job's restoration. The word "eyes" are mentioned in 27 verses in the Book of Job, and they are recorded from the Douay-Rheims 1899 American Edition known as DRA.

Job's Three Friends Come to See Him, Job 2:11 – 13
And when they had lifted up their eyes afar off, they knew him not, and crying out they wept, and rending their garments they sprinkled dust upon their heads toward heaven, Job 2:12.

Job's 1st Speech, Job 3:1 – 10
Because it shut not up the doors of the womb that bore me, nor took away evils from my eyes, Job 3:10.

Eliphaz First Speak to Job, Job 4:1 – 21
There stood one whose countenance I knew not, an image before my eyes, and I heard the voice as it were of a gentle wind, Job 4:16.

Job Cries Out to God, Job 7:6 – 21
Nor shall the sight of man behold me: they eyes are upon me, and I shall be no more, Job 7:8.

Job Plead to God, Job 10:1 – 22
Hast thou eyes of flesh: or, shalt thou see as man seeth, Job 10:4?

Zophar Says Job is Guilt and Deserves Punishment, Job 11:1 – 20
For thou hast said: My word is pure, and I am clean in thy sight. **PS:** Douay-Rheims 1899 American Edition (DRA) doesn't used the word "eyes" in Job 11:4; King James Version reads: For thou hast said, My doctrine is pure, and I am clean in thine eyes, Job 11:4.

But the eyes of the wicked shall decay, and the way to escape shall fail them, and their hope the abomination of the soul, Job 11:20.

The Life of Man, Job 14:1 – 6
And dost thou think it meet to open thy eyes upon such an one, and to bring him into judgment with thee, Job 14:3?

Eliphaz's Second Speech to Job, Job 15:1 – 35
Why doth thy heart elevate thee, and why dost thou stare with thy eyes, as if they were thinking great things, Job 15:12?

Job Replies: Miserable Comforters Are You, Job 16:1 – 22
My wrinkles bear witness against me, and a false speaker riseth up against my face, contradicting me. **PS:** Douay-Rheims 1899 American Edition (DRA) doesn't used the word "eyes" in Job 16:9; King James Version reads: He teareth me in his wrath, who hateth me: he gnasheth upon me with his teeth; mine enemy sharpeneth his eyes upon me, Job 16:9.

<u>Job's Hopes Have Died</u>, Job 17:1 – 16
He promiseth a prey to his companions, and the eyes of his children shall fail, Job 17:5.

<u>Job Answers His Friend, Bildad</u>, Job 19:1 – 29
Whom I myself shall see, and my eyes shall behold, and not another: this my hope is laid up in my bosom, Job 19:27.

<u>Job's 7th Speech is a Response to Zophar</u>, Job 21:1 – 34
Their seed continueth before them, a multitude of kindsmen, and of children's children in their sight. **PS:** Douay-Rheims 1899 American Edition (DRA) doesn't used the word "eyes" in Job 21:8; King James Version reads: Their seed is established in their sight with them, and their offspring before their eyes, Job 21:8.

His eyes shall see his own destruction, and he shall drink of the wrath of the Almighty, Job 21:20.

<u>Job Asked Why the Wicked Aren't Punished</u>, Job 24:1 – 25
God hath given him place for penance, and he abuseth it unto pride: but his eyes are upon his ways, Job 24:23.

<u>Job's View of the Wicked Fate</u>, Job 27:13 – 23
The rich man when he shall sleep shall take away nothing with him: he shall open his eyes and find nothing, Job 27:19.

<u>Where is Wisdom?</u> Job 28:12 – 28
It is hid from the eyes of all living. and the fowls of the air know it not, Job 28:21.

Job's Final Defense, Job 29:1 – 25
I was an eye to the blind, and a foot to the lame. **PS:** Douay-Rheims 1899 American Edition (DRA) doesn't used the word "eyes" in Job 29:15; King James Version reads: I was eyes to the blind, and feet was I to the lame, Job 29:15.

Job's Covenant, Job 31:1 – 16
I made a covenant with mine eyes, that I would not so much as think upon a virgin, Job 31:1?

If my step hath turned out of the way, and if my heart hath followed my eyes, and if a spot hath cleaved to my hands, Job 31:7.

If I have denied to the poor what they desired and have made the eyes of the widow to wait, Job 31:16.

Elihu Rebukes Job's 3 Friends, Job 32:1 – 22
So these three men ceased to answer Job, because he seemed just to himself. **PS:** Douay-Rheims 1899 American Edition (DRA) doesn't used the word "eyes" in Job 32:1; King James Version reads: So these three men ceased to answer Job, because he was righteous in his own eyes, Job 32:1.

Elihu Proclaim God's Justice, Job 34:1 – 37
For his eyes are upon the ways of men, and he considereth all their steps, Job 34:21.

God's Divine Discipline, Job 36:5 – 25
He with not take away his eyes from the just, and he placeth kings on the throne for ever, and they are exalted, Job 36:7.

Hawks and Eagles, Job 39:26 – 30
From thence she looketh for the prey, and her eyes behold afar off, Job 39:29.

The Lord Answers Job, Job 40:6 – 24
Shalt thou play with him as with a bird, or tie him up for thy handmaids? **PS:** Douay-Rheims 1899 American Edition (DRA) doesn't used the word "eyes" in Job 40:24; King James Version reads: He taketh it with his eyes: his nose pierceth through snares, Job 40:24.

God's Power in the Leviathan Creature, Job 41:1 – 34
For he shall esteem iron as straw, and brass as rotten wood. **PS:** Douay-Rheims 1899 American Edition (DRA) doesn't used the word "eyes" in Job 41:18; King James Version reads: By his neesings a light doth shine, and his eyes are like the eyelids of the morning, Job 41:18.

Note of Interests: Scholars believe that the Leviathan is a sea monster. Other scholars think it could be a whale, crocodile, or the Devil, Job 41:1, Psalms 74:14, and Isaiah 27:1. The word "Leviathan" is mentioned 5 times in 4 verses n the KJV Bible.

CHAPTER 11

LYRICAL POEMS

The Book of Psalms is a book of lyrical poems. Scholars believe it is the most widely read and highly treasured book in the Old Testament. Psalms is a collection of poems, hymns, and prayers that express the religious feelings of Jews throughout various periods of their biblical history. The Book of Psalms is described as the place to turn to when you are hurting.

Note of Interests: A lyric poem or lyrical poem is a poem in which the person usually expresses his private feelings and emotions. Lyric poems are typically spoken in the 1st person, and often displays strong emotions or romantic feelings. The term "lyric poem" comes from a form of Ancient Greek literature. The word "lyric" is defined by its musical accompaniment, which is usually on a stringed instrument known as a "lyre." A lyre is similar in appearance to a small harp, and the 1st among the string instruments to be invented. There are 3 categories of poetry, which are lyrical, dramatic, and epic.

The Book of Psalms has 150 psalms that communicate different thoughts regarding a psalmist's feeling, situation, or circumstance. Throughout the Book of Psalms, there is admiration, praise, and prayers to God, for God, and about God.

Note of Interests: The word "praise" is mentioned 214 times in the KJV Bible. It is mentioned the most in Psalms, a total of 130 times. The word "prayer" is also recorded the most in the Book of Psalms. Prayer is mentioned 128 times in the KJV Bible and 28 times in the Book of Psalms. However, the word "admiration" is only mentioned twice in the KJV; Jude 1:16 and Revelation 17:6 KJV.

The Book of Psalms covers approximately 1,000 years of history. The authors of Psalms are David, Asaph, the sons of Korah, Solomon, Heman the Ezrahite, Ethan the Ezrahite, and Moses. There are about 51 Psalms in which the author is unknown.

The Book of Psalms is divided into 5 sections. The reason(s) for the Book of Psalms division is uncertain. Jewish Midrash traditions suggest that the division is based on the 5 books of the Torah, which are Genesis, Exodus, Leviticus, Numbers, and Deuteronomy.

The Book of Genesis explains how God created the world, and how his relationship with man and the world begins. The Book of Exodus describes how God delivered Israel from slavery in Egypt and describes the special relationship Israel agrees to have with God. The Book of Leviticus is where God gives Israel instructions for how to serve and worship him. The Book of Numbers shows how Israel fails to trust and obey God and wandered in the wilderness for 40 years. The Book of Deuteronomy is where Moses gives Israel more instructions, repeats the law, and tells them to worship and obey God in the Promised Land.

The word "eyes" are mentioned in 42 verses in the Book of Psalms, and they are listed below.

Section 1: Psalms 1 – 41

Psalm 10:8
He sitteth in the lurking-places of the villages; In the secret places doth he murder the innocent; His eyes are privily set against the helpless. ASV

Psalm 11:4 – Psalm 11 written by David
Jehovah is in his holy temple; Jehovah, his throne is in heaven; His eyes behold, his eyelids try, the children of men. ASV

Psalm 13:3 – Psalm 13 written by David
Consider and hear me, O Jehovah my God: Lighten mine eyes, lest I sleep the sleep of death. ASV

Psalm 15:4 – Psalm 15 written by David
In whose eyes a reprobate is despised, But who honoreth them that fear Jehovah; He that sweareth to his own hurt, and changeth not. ASV

Psalm 17:2 – Psalm 17 written by David
Let my sentence come forth from thy presence; Let thine eyes look upon equity. ASV

Psalm 17:11
They have now compassed us in our steps; They set their eyes to cast us down to the earth. ASV

Psalm 19:8 – Psalm 19 written by David
The precepts of Jehovah are right, rejoicing the heart:
The commandment of Jehovah is pure, enlightening the
eyes. ASV

Psalm 25:15 – Psalm 25 written by David
Mine eyes are ever toward Jehovah; For he will pluck my
feet out of the net. ASV

Psalm 26:3 – Psalm 26 written by David
For thy lovingkindness is before mine eyes; And I have
walked in thy truth. ASV

Psalm 31:22 – Psalm 31 written by David
As for me, I said in my haste, I am cut off from before
thine eyes: Nevertheless thou heardest the voice of my
supplications, When I cried unto thee. ASV

Psalm 34:15 – Psalm 34 written by David
The eyes of Jehovah are toward the righteous, And his ears
are open unto their cry. ASV

Psalm 36:1 – Psalm 36 written by David
The transgression of the wicked saith within my heart,
There is no fear of God before his eyes. ASV

Psalm 36:2 – Psalm 36 written by David
For he flattereth himself in his own eyes, That his iniquity
will not be found out and be hated. ASV

Psalm 38:10 – Psalm 38 written by David
My heart throbbeth, my strength faileth me: As for the light
of mine eyes, it also is gone from me. ASV

Section 2: Psalms 42 – 72

Psalm 50:21 – Psalm 50 written by Asaph
These things hast thou done, and I kept silence; thou thoughtest that I was altogether such an one as thyself: but I will reprove thee, and set them in order before thine eyes. KJV

Psalm 66:7
He ruleth by his power for ever; his eyes behold the nations: let not the rebellious exalt themselves. Selah. KJV

Psalm 69:3 – Psalm 69 written by David
I am weary of my crying: my throat is dried: mine eyes fail while I wait for my God. KJV

Psalm 69:23
Let their eyes be darkened, that they see not; and make their loins continually to shake. KJV

Section 3: Psalms 73 – 89

Psalm 73:7 – Psalm 73 written by Asaph
Their eyes stand out with fatness, they exceed the imaginations of their heart. Darby

Psalm 77:4 – Psalm 77 written by Asaph
Thou holdest mine eyes waking: I am so troubled that I cannot speak. KJV

Section 4: Psalms 90 - 106

Psalm 91:8
Only with thine eyes shalt thou behold and see the reward of the wicked. KJV

Psalm 101:3 – Psalm 101 written by David
I will set no wicked thing before mine eyes: I hate the work of them that turn aside; it shall not cleave to me. KJV

Psalm 101:6
Mine eyes shall be upon the faithful of the land, that they may dwell with me: he that walketh in a perfect way, he shall serve me. KJV

Section 5: Psalms 107 - 150

Psalm 115:5
They have mouths, but they don't speak. The have eyes, but they don't see. WEB

Psalm 116:8
For you have delivered my soul from death, my eyes from tears, and my feet from failing. WEB

Psalm 118:23
This is Yahweh's doing. It is marvelous in our eyes. WEB

Psalm 119:18
Open my eyes, that I may see wondrous things out of your law. WEB

Psalm 119:37
Turn my eyes away from looking at worthless things. Revive me in your ways. WEB

Psalm 119:82
My eyes fail for your word. I say, "When will you comfort me?" WEB

Psalm 119:123
My eyes fail looking for your salvation, for your righteous word. WEB

Psalm 119:136
Streams of tears run down my eyes, because they don't observe your law. WEB

Psalm 119:148
My eyes stay open through the night watches, that I might meditate on your word. WEB

Note of Interests: Psalm 119 is the longest psalm with 176 verses. The greatness of God's word and the affliction of man are the major themes of Psalm119. The title given to this Psalm by scholars is "In Praise of the Law of the Lord." It is considered a written meditation of the "Law of the Lord" with many different facets.

The author of Psalm 119 is not mentioned, but most scholars believe that it was written by David, Ezra or Daniel. Throughout Psalm 119, he reflects on suffering and difficulties in his life. He mentioned plots, slanders, and taunts, and he speaks about persecutions, hardship, and afflictions.

The 119th chapter of Psalm is an alphabetic acrostic poem. There are 176 verses in Psalm 119 which is divided into 22 stanzas. One stanza is for each letter of the Hebrew alphabet, and each stanza has 8 verses. The Hebrew alphabet consists of 22 letters; 22 stanzas x 8 verses = 176 verses.

PS: The above "Note of Interests" was obtain from the book titled: Isaiah 26:3 – 4 "Perfect Peace XVIII" Midnight by Vanessa Rayner. *smile*

The word "eyes" is mentioned 6 times in Psalm 119, more than the other Psalms. Psalm 119 is the longest psalm, longest chapter in the Bible, and has more verses than 13 of the books in the Old Testament, and 16 books in the New Testament. Scholars believe that King David used Psalm 119 to teach his son, Solomon the alphabet and the statues of the God Israel serve.

Psalm 121:1
I will lift up my eyes to the hills. Where does my help come from? WEB

Psalm 123:1
To you I do lift I up my eyes, you who sit in the heavens. WEB

Psalm 123:2
Behold, as the eyes of servants look to the hand of their master, as the eyes of a maid to the hand of her mistress; so our eyes look to Yahweh, our God, until he has mercy on us. WEB

Psalm 131:1 – Psalm 131 written by David
Yahweh, my heart isn't haughty, nor my eyes lofty; nor do I concern myself with great matters, or things too wonderful for me. WEB

Psalm 132:4
I will not give sleep to my eyes, or slumber to mine eyelids. WEB

Psalm 135:16
They have mouths, but they can't speak. They have eyes, but they can't see. WEB

Psalm 139:16 – Psalm 139 written by David
Your eyes saw my body. In your book they were all written, the days that were ordained for me, when as yet there were none of them. WEB

Psalm 141:8 – Psalm 141 written by David
For my eyes are on you, Yahweh, the LORD. In you, I take refuge. Don't leave my soul destitute. WEB

Psalm 145:15 – Psalm 145 written by David
The eyes of all wait for you. You give them their food in due season. WEB

Psalm 146:8
Yahweh opens the eyes of the blind. Yahweh raises up those who are bowed down. Yahweh loves the righteous. WEB

CHAPTER 12

TO BE LIKE

The Book of Proverbs is one of the 5 Wisdom Books, which are also known as the Poetic Books of the Bible. There are 3 types of Hebrew poetry which are called lyric, didactic, and dramatic. Lyric poetry is accompanied by music, like the Book of Psalms. Didactic poetry teaches, entertains, and communicates basic principles of life, like Proverbs and Ecclesiastes. Dramatic poetry uses dialog fill with emotions and behavior to deliver its message, like the books of Job and Song of Solomon, also called Song of Songs.

The Book of Proverbs was written during Solomon's reign between 970 – 930 B.C. Solomon was born to King David and Bathsheba around 990 BC. Scholars believe, Solomon was 20 years old, when he began to reign, and shortly after he married the daughter of Pharaoh, the king of Egypt. She was his first wife of many more to come. Solomon had 700 wives and 300 concubines, 1 Kings 11:3.

King Solomon was known for his wealth, wisdom, and writings. The kingdom of Solomon extended from the Euphrates River in the north, to Egypt in the south. The building of the Holy Temple in Jerusalem is his greatest achievement, according to scholars.

The most famous demonstration of Solomon's wisdom occurred when 2 women came into his court with a baby, both claiming the baby belongs to them. The other woman killed her baby by accidentally smothering him. Solomon decision was to split the baby in half with a sword and give each woman half of the dead baby. The 1st woman was prepared to accept the decision, but the 2nd woman begged the King not to kill the baby but give the baby to the other woman. Solomon then knew the 2nd woman was the mother and gave the baby to her. One of Solomon most noticed visitor is the Queen of Sheba, named Makeda, who came from southern Arabia. She visited with Solomon for 6 months before she returned to her country. Queen of Sheba was extremely impressed by King Solomon's intellect,1 Kings 10, and 2 Chronicles 9.

According to the Bible, Solomon downfall came in his old age. He had many foreign wives, whom he allowed to worship other gods. He even built shrines for their sacrifices. The Prophet Ahijah of Shiloh prophesied that Jeroboam son of Nebat would become king over ten of the twelve tribes, instead of Solomon's son. Solomon was 80 years old when he died from natural causes.

The word "proverb" means "to be like." The Book of Proverbs is described as the book pack with godly wisdom for living a happy life. It contains timeless truth that is easy to understand and can be applied to your everyday life.

The Book of Proverbs begins with Solomon's advice to his son. According to 1 Kings 4:32, Solomon spoke 3,000 proverbs, but only 800 proverbs are included in the Book of Proverbs. He also wrote 1,005 songs. Scholars agree that Solomon wrote the book of Song of Songs, the Book of Proverbs, and the Book of Ecclesiastes.

The Book of Proverbs stresses that God must be respected, and His laws obeyed.

Solomon, the wisest king to ever rule, wrote most of the Book of Proverbs. Scholars believe that King Lemuel wrote Proverbs 31, the virtuous woman, and Agur wrote Proverbs 30, according to Proverbs 30:1. Other scholars believe that Lemuel and Agur are other names of King Solomon.

Note of Interests: The Babylonian Talmud states that 6 names were given to Solomon, which are Solomon, Jedidiah, Qoheleth, Ben lokoh, Agur, and Lemuel; Tractate Aboth, Chapter 5.

The Book of Proverbs has 31 chapters, and approximately 915 verses. Proverbs can be outlined as follows.

1. The Virtues of Wisdom, Chapters 1 – 9
2. The Proverbs of Solomon, Chapters 10 – 22:16
3. The Sayings of the Wise, Chapters 22:17 – 24
4. More Proverbs of Solomon, Chapters 25 – 29
5. The Words of Agur, Chapter 30
6. The Words of Lemuel, Chapter 31

The word "eyes" is mentioned in 30 verses, beginning in chapter 3.

<u>Seek Wisdom and Trust in the Lord</u>, Proverbs 3:1 – 35
Be not wise in thine own eyes: fear the LORD, and depart from evil, Proverbs 3:7.

My son, let not them depart from thine eyes: keep sound wisdom and discretion, Proverbs 3:21.

<u>A Father's Wise Instruction</u>, Proverbs 4:1 – 27

Let them not depart from thine eyes; keep them in the midst of thine hearts, Proverbs 4:21.

Let thine eyes look right on, and let thine eyelids look straight before thee, Proverbs 4:25.

Wisdom for Against Adultery, Proverbs 5:1 – 23
For the ways of man are before the eyes of the LORD, and he pondereth all his goings, Proverbs 5:21.

Wise Advice, Proverbs 6:1 – 19
Give not sleep to thine eyes, nor slumber to thine eyelids, Proverbs 6:4.

He winketh with his eyes, he speaketh with his feet, he teacheth with his fingers, Proverbs 6:13.

The Proverbs of Solomon, Proverbs 10:1 – 32
As vinegar to the teeth, and as smoke to the eyes, so is the sluggard to them that send him, Proverbs 10:26.

A Fool, Proverbs 12:15 – 16
The way of a fool is right in his own eyes: but he that hearkeneth unto counsel is wise, Proverbs 12:15.

The Lord Sees Everything, Proverbs 15:1 – 33
The eyes of the LORD are in every place, beholding the evil and the good, Proverbs 15:3.

The light of the eyes rejoiceth the heart: and a good report maketh the bones fat, Proverbs 15:30.

The Lord is the Judge of Our Motives, Proverbs 16:1 – 3

All the ways of a man are clean in his own eyes; but the LORD weigheth the spirits, Proverbs 16:2.

Don't Trust Violent People, Proverbs 16:29 – 33
He shutteth his eyes to devise froward things: moving his lips he bringeth evil to pass.

A Present, Proverbs 17:1 – 23
A gift is as a precious stone in the eyes of him that hath it: whithersoever it turneth, it prospereth, Proverbs 17:8.

Eyes of a Fool, Proverbs 17:24 – 28
Wisdom is before him that hath understanding; but the eyes of a fool are in the ends of the earth, Proverbs 17:24.

Separate the Evil from the Good, Proverbs 20:8 – 13
A king that sitteth in the throne of judgment scattereth away all evil with his eyes.

Love not sleep, lest thou come to poverty; open thine eyes, and thou shalt be satisfied with bread, Proverbs 20:13.

The Hearts, Proverbs 21:1 – 6
Every way of a man is right in his own eyes: but the LORD pondereth the hearts, Proverbs 21:2.

The Wicked, Proverbs 21:7 – 12
The soul of the wicked desireth evil: his neighbor findeth no favour in his eyes, Proverbs 21:10.

A Good Name, Proverbs 22:1 – 16
The eyes of the LORD preserve knowledge, and he overthroweth the words of the transgressor, Proverbs 22:12.

<u>Son, Listen to Your Father</u>, Proverbs 23:1 – 35
Wilt thou set thine eyes upon that which is not? For riches certainly make themselves wings; they fly away as an eagle toward heaven, Proverbs 23:5.

My son, give me thine heart, and let thine eyes observe my ways, Proverbs 23:26.

Who hath woe? Who hath sorrow? Who hath contentions? Who hath babbling? Who hath wounds without cause? Who hath redness of eyes, Proverbs 23:29?

Thine eyes shall behold strange women, and thine heart shall utter perverse things, Proverbs 23:33.

Note of Interests: In the Book of Proverbs, the word "eyes" are mentioned the most in Proverbs 23. A total of 4 times.

<u>Proverbs by Solomon Collected by King Hezekiah</u>, Proverbs 25:1 – 28
For better it is that it be said unto thee, Come up hither; than that thou shouldest be put lower in the presence of the prince whom thine eyes have seen, Proverbs 25:7.

Note of Interests: The phrase "thine eyes" are mentioned in 9 verses, out of 30 verses in the Book of Proverbs, and "the eyes" are mentioned in 8 verses. The phrase "his eyes" and "own eyes" are mentioned in 5 verses.

CHAPTER 13

THE LAST TWO POETIC BOOKS

Ecclesiastes and Song of Solomon are the last two poetry books of the Bible. Song of Solomon is also called the Song of Songs. Ecclesiastes and Song of Solomon are both packed with wisdom that seeks to reveal true happiness in life and true love in a relationship. The Book of Ecclesiastes has 12 chapters, while Song of Solomon has 8.

The word "Ecclesiastes" is a Latin title, which comes from the Greek word "ekklesiastes." It means "speaker in an assembly or church," traditionally the Ecclesiastes translated as "Teacher" or "Preacher." The writer of Ecclesiastes is a man who has allowed sin to consume him by being selfish, enjoying carnal, and sensual pleasures.

In the Book of Ecclesiastes, Solomon learns that real success can only be found in a right relationship with God. Solomon wrote Ecclesiastes around 935 BC. He wrote concerning the awareness of the mistakes that he made throughout his life. The Book of Ecclesiastes gives wisdom that will keep you from destroying your life. The word "eyes" is mentioned in 7 verses.

The Book of Ecclesiastes

Ecclesiastes has 12 chapters, a total of 222 verses, and 5,579 words, KJV. The main characters in the book is the Teacher and the Preacher. King Solomon repeatedly uses the phrase, "under the sun." A total of 27 times.

The Book of Ecclesiastes can be outlined as follow.

1. Life without God in Meaningless, Ecclesiastes 1:1 – 2:6
2. Life without God is Unfair and Full of Disappointments, Ecclesiastes 3:1 – 5:20
3. Life without God is Futility and Unfulfilling, Ecclesiastes 4:1 – 9:18
4. Life with God is True Fulfillment, Ecclesiastes 9:1 – 12

Does Hard Work Bring Happiness, Ecclesiastes 2:4 – 11
And whatsoever mine eyes desired I kept not from them; I withheld not my heart from any joy; for my heart rejoiced because of all my labour; and this was my portion from all my labour, Ecclesiastes 2:10 ASV.

Is Wisdom the Answer, Ecclesiastes 2:12 – 16
The wise man's eyes are in his head, but the fool walketh in darkness: and yet I perceived that one event happeneth to them all, Ecclesiastes 2:14 ASV.

Wealth Can't Buy Happiness, Ecclesiastes 5:10 – 17
When goods increase, they are increased that eat them; and what advantage is there to the owners thereof, save the beholding of them with their eyes, Ecclesiastes 5:11 ASV?

Life, Ecclesiastes 6:1 – 12
Better is the sight of the eyes than the wandering of the desire: this is also vanity and a striving after wind, Ecclesiastes 6:9 ASV.

<u>We Will Never Understand All God Doing</u>,
Ecclesiastes 8:11 - 17
When I applied my heart to know wisdom, and to see the business that is done upon the earth (for also there is that neither day nor night seeth sleep with his eyes), Ecclesiastes 8:16 ASV.

<u>Enjoy the Light of Day</u>, Ecclesiastes 11:7 – 10
Truly the light is sweet, and a pleasant thing it is for the eyes to behold the sun, Ecclesiastes 11:7 ASV.

Rejoice, O young man, in thy youth, and let thy heart cheer thee in the days of thy youth, and walk in the ways of thy heart, and in the sight of thine eyes; but know thou, that for all these things God will bring thee into judgment, Ecclesiastes 11:9 ASV.

Song of Solomon

The Book of Song of Songs is a collection of love poems written during Solomon's reign between 971 and 931 BC. The Book of Song of Songs is a dialogue between a young woman and her bridegroom, who is in love with her. The display of love between the young woman and her bridegroom represents the love that God has for His people. Solomon speaks about human attraction, romance, and sexual desires. The Book of Song of Solomon can be outlined in 6 main parts, which are listed below.

1. The Bride Expresses Her Desires to Her Beloved, Song of Songs 1:1 – 2:7
2. Intimate Affections Between the Bride and Groom, Song of Songs 2:8 – 3:5

3. The Engagement Takes Place, Song of Songs 3:6 – 5:1
4. The Bridegroom Goes Away for a Short Time, Song of Songs 5:2 – 6:9
5. The Bride Beauty is Described, Song of Songs 6:10 – 8:4
6. The Lovers Reunite in Love, Song of Songs 8:5 – 8:14

Note of Interests: Song of Songs is one of two books in the Bible that doesn't mention the word "God." The other book that doesn't mention "God" is Esther with 10 chapters.

Song of Songs has 8 chapters with 117 verses, and 2,658 words, KJV. The word "eyes" is mentioned 7 times.

The Man Speaks to the Woman He Loves,
Song of Solomon 1:1 – 17
Behold, thou art fair, my love; Behold, thou art fair: thine eyes are doves, Song of Solomon 1:15 Darby.

Solomon Admires His Bride's Beauty,
Song of Solomon 4:1 – 16
Behold, thou art fair, my love; behold, thou art fair; Thine eyes are doves behind thy veil; Thy hair is as a flock of goats, On the slopes of mount Gilead, Song of Solomon 4:1 Darby.

Thou hast ravished my heart, my sister, [my] spouse; Thou hast ravished my heart with one of thine eyes, With one chain of thy neck, Song of Solomon 4:9 Darby.

The Bride Praises Her Beloved, Song of Solomon 5:10 – 16
His eyes are like doves by the water-brooks, Washed with milk, fitly set, Song of Solomon 5:12 Darby.

<u>Praise of the Shulamite's Beauty</u>, Song of Solomon 6:4 – 10
Turn away thine eyes from me, For they overcome me. Thy hair is as a flock of goats On the slopes of Gilead, Song of Solomon 6:5 Darby.

Note of Interests: Many scholars consider "Shulamite" to be identical with "Shunammite;" an individual from a town called Shunem. Shunem was in the territory of Issachar, north of Jezreel and south of Mount Gilboa. The town is mentioned only three times in the Bible, Joshua 19:18, 1 Samuel 28:4, and 2 Kings 4:8. The Bible speak of two Shunammite women. According to 1 Kings 1, a young Shunammite named Abishag nursed and served King David in his old age. The other Shunammite woman, Elisha blessed her with a son in her old age, and later raise him from the dead when he died, 2 Kings 4:8 – 37.

<u>Her Beauty</u>, Song of Solomon 7:1 – 9
Thy neck is as a tower of ivory; Thine eyes, [like] the pools in Heshbon, By the gate of Bath-rabbim; Thy nose is like the tower of Lebanon, Which looketh toward Damascus, Solomon 7:4 Darby.

<u>The Woman</u>, Song of Solomon 8:10 – 12
I am a wall, and my breasts like towers; Then was I in his eyes as one that findeth peace, Song of Solomon 8:10 Darby.

The phrase "eyes are like doves" are mentioned in 3 of the 7 verses above; Song of Solomon 1:15, Song of Solomon 4:1, and Song of Solomon 5:12. In Song of Solomon 1:15 and Song of Solomon 4:1, Solomon is describing the eyes of his bride. Then in Song of Solomon 5:12, Solomon's bride is describing his eyes as "eyes are like a dove." In chapter 2, Solomon describes her voice as a dove, Song of Solomon 2:14.

My dove, in the clefts of the rock,
In the covert of the precipice, Let me see thy
countenance, let me hear they voice; For sweet
is thy voice, and thy countenance is comely.
Song of Solomon 2:14 Darby

Note of Interests: Jesus mentioned the word "dove" one times in the Bible, Matthew 10:16. Jesus told his disciples, he was sending them out as sheep amid wolves to preach the gospel, and to be wise as serpents and innocent as doves.

The dove does not soar like an eagle, nor attack like the hawk; it doesn't mimic words like the mockingbird, not as colorful as the cardinal, or have 3 eyelids like the owl. The dove is a peaceful, ordinary, innocent bird. It's the kind of bird that the poor people of Israel would offer for a sacrifice, Leviticus 12:8, Luke 2:24.

According to Matthew 3:16, John the Baptist said, after Jesus was baptized in the Jordan River, Jesus immediately came up from the water. He saw the heavens open, and then he saw the Spirit of God descending like a dove and lighting on Jesus. This biblical event is also mentioned in Mark 1, Luke 3, and John 1.

CHAPTER 14

THE BOOK OF ISAIAH

The Book of Isaiah is the 23rd book in the Old Testament. It's the first of the Major Prophet Books with 66 chapters, 1292 verses, and 25,608 words. The main message in the Book of Isaiah is "salvation," and it emphasizes salvation will come through the Messiah. The name "Isaiah" means "the LORD is salvation" in Hebrew.

Note of Interests: Isaiah from the Old Testament is the most quoted Prophet in the New Testament. He is referred to approximately 85 times in the New Testament. Jesus quoted from the Book of Isaiah 8 times.

King Hezekiah and his aides are believed to be the writers of the Book of Isaiah by many scholars. Other scholars believe Isaiah wrote chapters 1 – 39. However, it is widely accepted that the Prophet Isaiah did not write the entire Book of Isaiah.

The Prophet Isaiah was the son of Amoz, and he was born in Jerusalem and lived in Judah in the 8 BC. He was a descendant of the house of Judah. Isaiah lived about 700 years before the birth of Jesus Christ, during a time of great political turmoil, and the Assyrians had conquered Israel.

Isaiah received his calling as a prophet when he saw a vision of God in the temple in the year King Uzziah died, Isaiah

6:1. Isaiah describes the vision as the LORD sitting on the throne, high, and lofty; and the hem of His robe filled the temple. Standing above the LORD were the seraphs. They each had 6 wings, 2 covered their faces, 2 covered their feet, and 2 were used for flying. The seraphs called one to another, "Holy, holy, holy is the LORD of hosts." One of the seraphs took a hot burning coal from the altar and flew to Isaiah and touched his mouth with it. Immediately, Isaiah heard the voice of the LORD saying, "Whom shall I send, and who will go for us?" Isaiah quickly said, "Here am I; send me."

Note of Interests: Isaiah's contemporaries were the Prophets Amos, Hosea, and Micah. Amos prophesied around 760 BC; it was explicitly to Israel, not Judah. He predicted the overthrow of Israel by the Assyrians. Hosea lived and prophesied during the reigns of the last 2 kings of Israel, just before the destruction of Israel in 722 BC by the Assyrian. He spoke of the desolations that would result from being unfaithful to God. Micah prophesied the fall of Samaria which took place around 722 BC. He also prophesied that Israel and Judah would be punished for idolatry, injustice, and immorality. Micah also spoke of redemption.

Isaiah ministry lasts approximately 50 years, during Isaiah lifetime, he prophesied during the reign of 4 kings, who were Uzziah (Azariah), Jotham, Ahaz, and Hezekiah. Isaiah proclaimed a message of repentance from sin. He denounced the riches of the wealthy who were gained by oppressing the poor.

Isaiah is known as the Hebrew Prophet, who prophesied the coming of Jesus Christ to save humankind from sin. He spoke of Jesus' virgin birth, rejection, and death. He prophesied the Jews dispersion, persecution, and eventual return back to Jerusalem. Isaiah foretells the Babylonian Empire being permanently overthrown, and this happened in 539 BC, approximately 200 years after he was born.

Isaiah's persecutors sawed him in half. According to oral Rabbinical tradition, Isaiah was executed by his grandson, King Manasseh, the son of King Hezekiah. Isaiah was accused of being a false prophet, and execution was the judgment for false prophets. The Prophet Isaiah was hiding in a hollow tree, so one of the soldiers had it sawed in half.

The word "eyes" is mentioned 37 times in 36 verses in the Book of Isaiah. They are listed below, in the King James Version with a subject title.

Prophecies, Judgment, and Promise, Chapters 1 – 39

The Wickedness of Judah, Isaiah 1:1 – 20
And when ye spread forth your hands, I will hide mine eyes from you: yea, when ye make many prayers, I will not hear: your hands are full of blood, Isaiah 1:15.

Wash you, make you clean; put away the evil of your doings from before mine eyes; cease to do evil, Isaiah 1:16.

God Will Punish Judah, Isaiah 3:1 – 15
For Jerusalem is ruined, and Judah is fallen: because their tongue and their doings are against the LORD, to provoke the eyes of his glory, Isaiah 3:8.

A Warning to Jerusalem, Isaiah 3:16 – 26
Moreover the LORD saith, Because the daughters of Zion are haughty, and walk with stretched forth necks and wanton eyes, walking and mincing as they go, and making a tinkling with their feet, Isaiah 3:16.

Judah's Judgment, Isaiah 5:8 – 30
And the mean man shall be brought down, and the mighty man shall be humbled, and the eyes of the lofty shall be humbled, Isaiah 5:15.

Woe unto them that are wise in their own eyes, and prudent in their own sight, Isaiah 5:21!

Isaiah's Vision of the LORD in the Temple, Isaiah 6:1 – 13
Then said I, Woe is me! For I am undone; because I am a man of unclean lips, and I dwell in the midst of people of unclean lips: for mine eyes have seen the King, the LORD of hosts, Isaiah 6:5.

Make the heart of this people fat, and make their ears heavy, and shut their eyes; lest they see with their eyes, and hear with their ears, and understand with their hearts, and covert, and be healed, Isaiah 6:10.

A Rod from the Stem of Jesse, Isaiah 11:1 – 16
And shall make him of quick understanding in the fear of the LORD: and he shall not judge after the sight of his eyes, neither reprove after the hearing of his ears, Isaiah 11:3.

A Prophecy Against Babylon, Isaiah 13:1 – 22
Their children also shall be dashed to pieces before their eyes; their houses shall be spoiled, and their wives ravished, Isaiah 13:16.

Their bows also shall dash the young men to pieces; and they shall have no pity on the fruit of the womb; their eyes shall not spare children, Isaiah 13:18.

Isaiah's Proclamation Against Damascus, Isaiah 17:1 – 14
At that day shall a man look to his Maker, and his eyes shall have respect to the Holy One of Israel, Isaiah 17:7.

God Warning to Jerusalem, Isaiah 29:1 – 14
For the LORD hath poured out upon you the spirit of deep sleep, and hath closed your eyes: the prophets and your rulers, the seers hath he covered, Isaiah 29:10.

A Better Time is Coming, Isaiah 29:17 – 24
And in that day shall the deaf hear the words of the book, and the eyes of the blind shall see out of obscurity, and out of darkness, Isaiah 29:18.

The LORD Will Hear His People Cry, Isaiah 30:19 – 33
And though the LORD gives you the bread of adversity, and the water of affliction, yet shall not thy teachers be removed into a corner any more, but thine eyes shall see thy teachers, Isaiah 30:20.

A King Reigning in Righteousness is Coming, Isaiah 32:1 – 8
And the eyes of them that see shall not be dim, and the ears
of them that hear shall hearken, Isaiah 32:3.

O LORD, Be Gracious to Us, Isaiah 33:1 – 19
He that walketh righteously, and speaketh uprightly; he that
despiseth the gain of oppressions, that shaketh his hands
from holding of bribes, that stoppeth his ears from hearing
of blood, and shutteth his eyes from seeing evil, Isaiah 33:15.

Thine eyes shall see the king in his beauty: they shall behold
the land this is very far off, Isaiah 33:17.

The LORD Will Protect Jerusalem, Isaiah 33:20 – 24
Look upon Zion, the city of our solemnities: thine eyes shall
see Jerusalem a quiet habitation, a tabernacle that shall not
be taken down; not one of the stakes thereof shall ever be
removed, neither shall any of the cords thereof be broken,
Isaiah 33:20.

Zion's Fruitful Future, Isaiah 35:1 – 10
Then the eyes of the blind shall be opened, and the ears of
the deaf shall be unstopped, Isaiah 35:5.

Hezekiah Prayed to the LORD, Isaiah 37:14 – 20
Incline thine ear, O LORD, and hear; open thine eyes, O
LORD, and see: and hear all the words of Sennacherib,
which hath sent to reproach the living God, Isaiah 37:17.

The LORD Answers Hezekiah Through Isaiah,
Isaiah 37:21 – 33
Whom hast thou reproached and blasphemed? And against whom hast thou exalted thy voice, and lifted up thine eyes on high? Even against the Holy One of Israel, Isaiah 37:23.

King Hezekiah's Song of Praise After He Was Healed,
Isaiah 38:1 – 20
Like a crane of a swallow, so did I chatter: I did mourn as a dove: mine eyes fail with looking upward: O LORD, I am oppressed; undertake for me, Isaiah 38:14.

The Deliverance and Restoration of Israel, Chapter 40 – 66

God Rules the Whole Earth, Isaiah 40:21 – 26
Lift up your eyes on high, and behold who hath created these things, that bringeth out their host by number: he calleth them all by names by the greatness of his might, for that he is strong in power; not one faileth, Isaiah 40:26.

The LORD's Servant, Isaiah 42:1 – 9
To open the blind eyes, to bring out the prisoners from the prison, and them that sit in darkness out of the prison house, Isaiah 42:7.

The LORD Alone is God, Isaiah 43:8 – 13
Bring forth the blind people that have eyes, and the deaf that have ears, Isaiah 43:8.

I Am the First and the Last, Isaiah 44:6 – 23
They have not known nor understood: for he hath shut their eyes, that they cannot see; and their hearts, that they cannot understand, Isaiah 44:18.

The Servant of the LORD, Isaiah 49:1 – 7
And now, saith the LORD that formed me from the womb to be his servant, to bring Jacob again to him, Though Israel be not gathered, yet shall I be glorious in the eyes of the LORD, and my God shall be my strength, Isaiah 49:5.

The Day of Salvation, Isaiah 49:8 – 26
Lift up thine eyes round about, and behold: all these gather themselves together, and come to thee. As I live, saith the LORD, thou shalt surely clothe thee with them all, as with an ornament, and bind them on thee, as a bride doeth, Isaiah 49:18.

Everlasting Salvation, Isaiah 51:1 – 16
Lift up your eyes to the heavens, and look upon the earth beneath: for the heavens shall vanish away like smoke, and the earth shall wax old like a garment, and they that dwell therein shall die in like manner: but my salvation shall be for ever, and my righteousness shall not be abolished, Isaiah 51:6.

The LORD Saves Israel, Isaiah 52:1 – 11
The LORD hath made bare his holy arm in the eyes of all the nations; and all the ends of the earth shall see the salvation of our God, Isaiah 52:10.

Sin Brings Disorder, Isaiah 59:9 – 21
We grope for the wall like the blind, and we grope as if we had no eyes: we stumble at noon day as in the night; we are in desolate places as dead men, Isaiah 59:10.

A New Day for Jerusalem, Isaiah 60:1 – 22
Lift up thine eyes round about, and see: all they gather themselves together, they come to thee: thy sons shall come from far, and thy daughters shall be nursed at thy side, Isaiah 60:4.

The LORD's Judgment and Salvation, Isaiah 65:1 – 16
Therefore will I number you to the sword, and ye shall all bow down to the slaughter: because when I called, ye did not answer; when I spake, ye did not hear; but did evil before mine eyes, and did choose that wherein I delighted not, Isaiah 65:12.

That he who blesseth himself in the earth shall bless himself in the God of truth; and he that sweareth in the earth shall swear by the God of truth; because the former troubles are forgotten, and because they are hid from mine eyes, Isaiah 65:16.

Thus Says The LORD, Isaiah 66:1 – 13
I also will choose their delusions, and will bring their fears upon them; because when I called, none did answer; when I spake, they did not hear: but they did evil before mine eyes, and chose that in which I delighted not, Isaiah 66:4.

CHAPTER 15

THE BOOKS OF JEREMIAH & LAMENTATIONS

The Book of Jeremiah is the 2nd Major Prophet Book written between 630 and 580 BC. The Book of Jeremiah records the final prophecies against Judah's sins. God allowed the Babylonians to besiege, plunder, burn and destroy the beautiful city of Jerusalem because of Judah's continued and unrepentant idolatry.

Lamentations were written by Jeremiah, after soldiers from Babylon destroyed Jerusalem around 586 BC, and led the people into captivity. Lamentations consist of poetic laments describing the anguish over Jerusalem receiving God's judgment.

Jeremiah sadly recounts and reflects on his personal experience during the destruction of Jerusalem. He stresses to God's people that those who disrespect Him will be judged and punished. He expresses his profound sorrow as well as compassion and empathy for God's nation as it is left in ruins.

Note of Interests: Babylon was God's instrument of judgment upon Judah. Though the punishment was severe, God didn't allow His chosen people to be obliterated only because of the love he had for them then and still has for them, today.

Jeremiah was the son of Hilkiah, who was a priest, and they lived in Anathoth. Jeremiah was raised in a Levitical tribe, and he knew the law of the LORD, as well as, the temple and priesthood ordinances, exceptionally well. Scholars believe Jeremiah was 17 years old when he received his calling from the LORD. Jeremiah did not marry or have any children because he was forbidden by the LORD, Jeremiah 16:2.

Note of Interests: The word "Levitical" is derived from the Israelite tribe of Levi. The Tribe of Levi descended from Levi, the 3rd son of Jacob and Leah. A Levite is a Jewish male descended from the Tribe of Levi. The Levitical priesthood begins with Aaron, who was the older brother of Moses, Exodus 28:1- 3. They ministered in the tabernacle, and later in the temple. They were mediators between man and God and offered sacrifices for the people required by the Mosaic Law. Other well-known Levitical priests in the Bible are Ezra, Eli, and John the Baptist's father named Zechariah.

When Jeremiah was appointed by the LORD to preach against the sins of the people and tell of the coming judgment, he resisted. He told the LORD; he was only a child and did not know how to speak. The LORD then touched Jeremiah's mouth to place His words there.

Afterward, Jeremiah became a faithful, God-fearing man who preached for 40 years. He was known as the "weeping prophet" because he cried tears of sadness over the sins of the people, the destruction of the city, and the future desolation that was going to happen to his people, Jeremiah 9:1, Jeremiah 13:17.

God sent Jeremiah to give Judah the last warning before He cast them out of the land. Jeremiah, the last prophet that God sent to preach to the southern kingdom, which consisted of the tribes of Judah and Benjamin.

Note of Interests: Jesus Christ will also weep over Jerusalem, 6 centuries later, Matthew 23:37 – 38.

Although the Prophet Jeremiah was faithful to the LORD, he suffered all kinds of mistreatment, persecution, hardships, and trials; several are listed below.

1. The temple chief named Pashhur had Jeremiah beaten and put in chains at the upper Benjamin Gate in the LORD's Temple, Jeremiah 20:1 – 6.
2. Jeremiah's fellow Jews tried to have him executed after he preached the LORD would destroy the temple like he destroyed Shiloh if they didn't repent, Jeremiah 26:7 - 24.
3. Jeremiah dealt with the false prophet Hananiah prophesying lies to the people. Hananiah prophesied that Israel would defeat King Nebuchadnezzar of Babylon, which wasn't true, Jeremiah 28:1 – 17.
4. King Jehoiakim of Judah burns the first scroll that the LORD told Jeremiah to send to him, telling the people of Israel to stop sinning, and turn back to Him, Jeremiah 36:1 – 26.
5. Jeremiah prophesied to the people of Judah, if they surrender to the Babylonians, they would live. Shephatiah, Gedaliah, Jehucal, and Pashhur had Jeremiah was thrown down a well that belongs to Malchiah, the king's son, and left to die in the

mud. Ebedmelech from Ethiopia an official at the palace spoke with King Zedekiah, and the king permitted him to remove Jeremiah out of the well, Jeremiah 38:1 – 13.

6. Jeremiah was accused of lying to those who consulted him, by Azariah Johanan, Jeremiah 43:1 – 13.

The Book of Jeremiah has 52 chapters, and 1,366 verses and the word "eyes" is mentioned 28 times in 25 verses. The verses are recorded from the World English Bible (WEB), along with a subject title.

The Book of Jeremiah

Judah is Unfaithful, Jeremiah 3:1 – 5
Lift up your eyes to the bare heights, and see! Where have you not been lain with? You have sat waiting for them by the road, as an Arabian in the wilderness. You have polluted the land with your prostitution and with your wickedness, Jeremiah 3:2.

Jerusalem Refused to Repent to the LORD, Jeremiah 5:1 – 13
O Yahweh, don't your eyes look on truth? You have stricken them, but they were not grieved. You have consumed them, but they have refused to receive correction. They have made their faces harder than a rock. They have refused to return, Jeremiah 5:3.

The LORD Proclaims Judgment on Jerusalem,
Jeremiah 5:14 – 31
Hear now this, foolish people, and without understanding; who have eyes, and don't see; who have ears, and don't hear, Jeremiah 5:21.

Jeremiah's Sermon at the Temple, Jeremiah 7:1 – 34
Has this house, which is called by my name, become a den of robbers in your eyes? Behold, I, even I, have seen it, says Yahweh, Jeremiah 7:11.

Disobedience Brings God's Judgment on Judah, Jeremiah 9:1 – 17
Oh, that my head were waters, and my eyes a spring of tears, that I might weep day and night for the slain of the daughter of my people, Jeremiah 9:1!

The People Mourn, Jeremiah 9:17 – 26
And let them make haste, and take up a wailing for us, that our eyes may run down with tears, and our eyelids gush out with waters, Jeremiah 9:18.

Judah Warning Against Pride, Jeremiah 13:15 – 27
Lift up your eyes, and see those who come from the north: where is the flock that was given you, your beautiful flock, Jeremiah 13:20?

Judah's Drought, Jeremiah 14:1 – 10
The wild donkeys stand on the bare heights, they pant for air like jackals; their eyes fail, because there is no herbage, Jeremiah 14:6.

The LORD Forbids Jeremiah to Intercede for Judah, Jeremiah 14:11 – 18
You shall say this word to them, Let my eyes run down with tears night and day, and let them not cease; for the virgin daughter of my people is broken with a great breach, with a very grievous wound, Jeremiah 14:17.

Judah's Future Punishment, Jeremiah 16:5 – 13
For Yahweh of Armies, the God of Israel says: Behold, I will cause to cease out of this place, before your eyes and in your days, the voice of mirth and the voice of gladness, the voice of the bridegroom and the voice of the bride, Jeremiah 16:9.

The LORD Will Restore, Jeremiah 16:14 – 21
For my eyes are upon all their ways; they are not hidden from my face, neither is their iniquity concealed from my eyes, Jeremiah 16:17.

Pashhur, the Priest Struck Jeremiah, Jeremiah 20:1 - 6
For Yahweh says, Behold, I will make you a terror to yourself, and to all thy friends; and they shall fall by the sword of their enemies, and your eyes shall see it; and I will give all Judah into the hand of the king of Babylon, and he shall carry them captive into Babylon, and shall kill them with the sword, Jeremiah 20:4.

Judgement Against King Jehoiakim of Judah,
Jeremiah 22:13 – 23
But your eyes and your heart are not but for your covetousness, and for shedding innocent blood, and for oppression, and for violence, to do it, Jeremiah 22:17.

The Good and Bad Figs, Jeremiah 24:1 – 10
For I will set my eyes on them for good, and I will bring them again to this land: and I will build them, and not pull them down; and I will plant them, and not pluck them up, Jeremiah 24:6.

Jeremiah's Letter to the Exiles in Babylon, Jeremiah 29:1 – 23
Yahweh of Armies, the God of Israel, says concerning Ahab the
son of Kolaiah, and concerning Zedekiah the son of Maaseiah,
who prophesy a lie to you in my name: Behold, I will deliver
them into the hand of Nebuchadnezzar king of Babylon; and
he shall kill them before your eyes, Jeremiah 29:21.

Rachel's Sadness Turns to Joy, Jeremiah 31:15 – 40
Yahweh says: Refrain your voice from weeping, and your
eyes from tears; for your work shall be rewarded, says
Yahweh; and they shall come again from the land of the
enemy, Jeremiah 31:16.

Jeremiah Buys A Field, Jeremiah 32:1 – 15
And Zedekiah king of Judah shall not escape out of the hand
of the Chaldeans but shall surely be delivered into the hand
of the king of Babylon, and shall speak with him mouth to
mouth, and his eyes shall see his eyes, Jeremiah 32:4.

Jeremiah's Prayer, Jeremiah 32:16 – 25
Great in counsel, and mighty in work; whose eyes are open to
all the ways of the sons of men, to give everyone according to his
ways, and according to the fruit of his doings, Jeremiah 32:19.

A Warning for King Zedekiah, Jeremiah 34:1 – 7
And you shall not escape out of the hand, but shall surely be
taken, and delivered into his hand; and your eyes shall see
the eyes of the king of Babylon, and he shall speak with you
mouth to mouth, and you shall go to Babylon, Jeremiah 34:3.

Jerusalem Captive by the Babylonians, Jeremiah 39:1 – 10
Then the king of Babylon killed the sons of Zedekiah in Riblah before his eyes: also the king of Babylon killed all the nobles of Judah, Jeremiah 39:6.

Moreover, he put out Zedekiah's eyes, and bound him in fetters, to carry him to Babylon, Jeremiah 39:7.

Jeremiah Plead the People Case Before the LORD, Jeremiah 42:1 – 22
And said to Jeremiah the prophet, Please let our supplication be presented before you, and pray for us to Yahweh your God, even for all this remnant; for we are left but a few of many, as your eyes do see us, Jeremiah 42:2.

The Fall of Jerusalem Recounted, Jeremiah 52:1 – 11
He did that which was evil in Yahweh's sight, according to all that Jehoiakim had one, Jeremiah 52:2. The KJV reads, "And he did that which was evil in the eyes of the LORD, according to all that Jehoiakim had done."

The king of Babylon killed the sons of Zedekiah before his eyes: he killed also all the princes of Judah in Riblah, Jeremiah 52:10.

He put out the eyes of Zedekiah; and the king of Babylon bound him in fetters, and carried him to Babylon, and put him in prison until the day of his death, Jeremiah 52:11.

The Book of Lamentations

The Book of Lamentations is the 25th book in the Bible. It has 5 chapters, 154 verses, and 3,415 words. Lamentations consist of 5 chapters, which can also be called 5 "songs of sorrow." They are described below.

Chapter 1   -   The Destruction of Jerusalem
Chapter 2   -   The Anger of God
Chapter 3   -   The Prayer for Mercy
Chapter 4   -   The Siege of Jerusalem
Chapter 5   -   The Prayer of Restoration

The word "eyes" is mentioned 3 times among the 5 "songs of sorrow" beginning with chapter 2. Those verses are recorded from the Douay-Rheims 1899 American Edition (DRA) with a subject title.

<u>The LORD in His Anger</u>, Lamentations 2:1 – 22
Caph. My eyes have failed with weeping, my bowels are troubled: my liver is poured out upon the earth, for the destruction of the daughter of my people, when the children, and the sucklings fainted away in the streets of the city, Lamentations 2:11.

<u>The Babylonian's Siege Described</u>, Lamentations 4:1 – 22
Ain. While we were yet standing, our eyes failed, expecting help for us in vain, when we looked attentively towards a nation that was not able to save, Lamentations 4:17.

<u>A Prayer for Mercy</u>, Lamentations 5:1 – 22
Therefore, is our heart sorrowful, therefore are our eyes become dim, Lamentations 5:17.

CHAPTER 16

THE LAST TWO MAJOR PROPHET BOOKS

Ezekiel and Daniel are the authors of the last two Major Prophet Books. The books of Ezekiel and Daniel were written during the Babylonian captivity of the Jews. Ezekiel ministered to his people in exile, and Daniel served in the royal court of Nebuchadnezzar, King of Babylon. The name Ezekiel means "strengthened by God" and Daniel name means "God is my judge."

The Prophet Ezekiel was the son of a priest named Buzi. He belongs to the family of Zadok, who was also a priest. Ezekiel was raised in Jerusalem and served as a priest in the temple. Ezekiel ministered during the same time Jeremiah. Jeremiah was still in Judah ministering, while Ezekiel was with the exiles.

Ezekiel was among the 2nd group of captives taken to Babylon after Jerusalem was defeated. While in Babylon he became a prophet for God. Ezekiel received his call from the LORD by a vision. The LORD told Ezekiel he was sending him to speak to His stubborn and hard-headed people. The LORD then told Ezekiel to open his mouth to eat a scroll with words on both sides, which tasted sweet as honey.

Nebuchadnezzar's armies exiled 3,000 Jews from Judah around 598 BC.

Ezekiel and his wife lived on the banks of the Chebar River, in Tel Abib with other exiles from Judah. According to Ezekiel 24, Ezekiel's wife died on the day of the final seize of Jerusalem.

Note of Interests: Ezekiel was the 1st prophet to be called by the LORD outside of Israel during the Babylonian Captivity.

Ezekiel begins his prophetic ministry around 593 BC before the final destruction of Jerusalem. He preached about condemnation and judgment concerning the unfaithfulness and rebellious people of the nation, Judah. After the destruction of Jerusalem, Ezekiel prophesied hope for the future of Judah and Israel. He announced God's impending judgment upon the nations that surrounded Judah and stressed that God would re-establish and restore Israel in the future.

The Book of Ezekiel is the 26th book of the Bible. It has 48 chapters and 1272 verses. The first part of the Book of Ezekiel mentions the sin of Judah and the judgment of God. Ezekiel describes how God will destroy Jerusalem in chapters 1 – 24. According to Ezekiel 25 – 32, Ezekiel prophesied the punishment of the surrounding nations. In chapters 33 – 39 of Ezekiel, he speaks on God's future for Israel, and God will bring Israel back to their country. The last part of the Book of Ezekiel chapters 40 – 48 describes the future temple and sacrifices. In the Book of Ezekiel, the word "eyes" is mentioned 28 times in 27 verses, and they are listed below from the King James Version with a subject title.

The Book of Ezekiel

<u>Ezekiel 1st Vision by the River Chebar – God's Throne</u>, Ezekiel 1:1 – 28
As for their rings, they were so high that they were dreadful; and their rings were full of eyes round about them four, Ezekiel 1:18.

<u>Ezekiel' Prophecies Against Israel</u>, Ezekiel 6:1 – 14
And they that escape of you shall remember me among the nations whither they shall be carried captives, because I am broken with their whorish heart, which hath departed from me, and with their eyes, which go a whoring after their idols: and they shall lothe themselves for the evils which they have committed in all their abominations, Ezekiel 6:9.

<u>Ezekiel 2nd Vision – The Sins of Jerusalem</u>, Ezekiel 8:1 – 18
Then said he unto me, Son of man, lift up thine eyes now the way toward the north, So I lifted up mine eyes the way toward the north, and behold northward at the gate of the altar this image of jealousy in the entry, Ezekiel 8:5.

<u>The Glory of the LORD Leave the Temple</u>, Ezekiel 10:1 – 22
And their whole body, and their backs, and their hands, and their wings, and the wheels, were full of eyes round about, even the wheels that they 4 had, Ezekiel 10:12.

<u>Ezekiel Acts Out Israel's Captivity</u>, Ezekiel 12:1 – 16
Son of man, thou dwellest in the midst of a rebellious house, which have eyes to see, and see not; they have ears to hear, and hear not: for they are a rebellious house, Ezekiel 12:2.

And the prince that is among them shall bear upon his shoulder in the twilight and shall go forth: they shall dig through the wall to carry out thereby: he shall cover his face, the he see not the ground with his eyes, Ezekiel 12:12.

<u>Sins of Parents and Children</u>, Ezekiel 18:1 – 32
And hath not eaten upon the mountains, neither hath lifted up his eyes to the idols of the house of Israel, neither hath defiled his neighbour's wife, neither hath come near to a menstruous woman, Ezekiel 18:6.

Hath oppressed the poor and needy, hath spoiled by violence, hath not restored the pledge, and hath lifted up his eyes to the idols, hath committed abomination, Ezekiel 18:12.

That hath not eaten upon the mountains, neither hath lifted up his eyes to the idols of the house of Israel, hath not defiled his neighbour's wife, Ezekiel 18:15.

<u>Israel Continue to Rebel Against the LORD</u>, Ezekiel 20:1 – 32
Then said I unto them, Cast ye away every man the abominations of his eyes, and defile not yourselves with the idols of Egypt: I am the LORD your God, Ezekiel 20:7.

But they rebelled against me, and would not hearken unto me: they did not every man cast away the abominations of their eyes, neither did they forsake the idols of Egypt: then I said, I will pour out my fury upon them, to accomplish my anger against them in the midst of the land of Egypt, Ezekiel 20:8.

Because they had not executed my judgments, but had despised my statues, and had polluted my sabbaths, and their eyes were after their fathers' idols, Ezekiel 20:24.

The LORD Will Punish Jerusalem, Ezekiel 21:1 – 7
Sigh therefore, thou son of man, with the breaking of thy loins; and with bitterness sigh before their eyes, Ezekiel 21:6.

The LORD is Furious, Ezekiel 22:23 – 31
Her priests have violated my law, and have profaned mine holy things: they have put no difference between the holy and profane, neither have they shewed difference between the unclean and the clean, and have hid their eyes from my sabbaths, and I am profaned among them, Ezekiel 22:26.

Two Sinful Sisters, Oholah and Oholibah, Ezekiel 23:1 - 21
And as soon as she saw the with her eyes, she doted upon them, and sent messengers unto them into Chaldea, Ezekiel 23:16.

The LORD Will Punish Oholibah, Ezekiel 23:22 – 35
Thus will I make thy lewdness to cease from thee, and thy whoredom brought from the land of Egypt: so that thou shalt not lift up thine eyes unto them, nor remember Egypt any more, Ezekiel 23:27.

Judgment on Oholah and Oholibah Ezekiel 23:36 – 49
And furthermore, that ye have sent for men to come from far, unto whom a messenger was sent; and, lo, they came: for whom thou didst wash thyself, paintedest thy eyes, and deckedst thyself with ornaments, Ezekiel 23:40.

Ezekiel's Wife Dies Suddenly, Ezekiel 24:15 – 27
Son of man, behold, I take away from thee the desire of
thine eyes with a stroke: yet neither shalt thou mourn nor
weep, neither shall they tears run down, Ezekiel 24:16.

Speak unto the house of Israel, Thus said the LORD God;
Behold, I will profane my sanctuary, the excellency of your
strength, the desire of your eyes, and that which your soul
pitieth; and your sons and your daughters whom ye have left
shall fall by the sword, Ezekiel 24:21.

Also, thou son of man, shall it not be in the day when I take
from them their strength, the joy of their glory, the desire
of their eyes, and that whereupon they set their minds, their
sons and their daughters, Ezekiel 24:25.

The News of Jerusalem Fall, Ezekiel 33:21 – 30
Wherefore say unto them, Thus saith the LORD God; Ye
eat with the blood, and lift up your eyes toward your idols,
and shed blood: and shall ye possess the land, Ezekiel 33:25?

For the Sake of His Holy Name, Ezekiel 36:22 – 38
And I will sanctify my great name, which was profaned
among the heathen, which ye have profaned in the midst
of them; and the heathen shall know that I am the LORD,
saith the LORD God, when I shall be sanctified in you
before your eyes, Ezekiel 36:23.

The Valley of the Dry Bones, Ezekiel 37:1 – 28
And the sticks whereon thou writest shall be in thine hand
before their eyes, Ezekiel 37:20.

Prophecy Against Gog, A Chief Prince, Ezekiel 38:1 – 23
And thou shalt come up against my people of Israel, as a cloud to
cover the land; it shall be in the latter days, and I will bring thee
against my land, that the heathen may know me, when I shall
be sanctified in thee, O Gog, before their eyes, Ezekiel 38:16.

Thus will I magnify myself, and sanctify myself; and I will
be known in the eyes of many nations, and they shall know
that I am the LORD, Ezekiel 38:23.

The Book of Daniel

The biblical events surrounding Daniel began when Daniel
and other young boys by the names of Hananiah, Mishael, and
Azariah from Judah were taken captive by King Nebuchadnezzar
of Babylon, Daniel 1 – 4. Scholars believe Daniel, Hananiah,
Mishael, and Azariah were about 14 years old.

Note of Interests: King Nebuchadnezzar's chief official changed
Daniel, Hananiah, Mishael, and Azariah names to Babylonian
names that related to Babylonian deities. Belteshazzar was
Daniel new name, which means "Bel protects his life." Bel
was the name of the god whom Nebuchadnezzar worshipped.
Hananiah name was changed to Shadrach, which relates to the
"Sun-god." Mishael name was changed to Meshach, which
relates to the goddess of "Venus." Abednego was Azariah new
name, which means "servant of Nego," who was another false
god of the Babylonian, Daniel 1:1 – 7. **PS:** If you like to know
what Daniel, Hananiah, Mishael, and Azariah's names mean
in the Hebrew Language; they're in the back of the book. Smile

The Book of Daniel is the last book of the Major Prophet Books. It is the 27th book in the Bible, and has 12 chapters, and approximately 357 verses. The word "eyes" is mentioned 7 times in 6 verses. They are listed below in the KJV.

Nebuchadnezzar Praises God, Daniel 4:34 – 37
And at the end of the days I Nebuchadnezzar lifted up mine eyes unto the heaven, and mine understanding returned unto me, and I blessed the most High, and I praised and honoured him that liveth for ever, whose dominion is an everlasting dominion, and his kingdom is from generation to generation, Daniel 4:34.

Daniel's Vision of the 4 Beasts, Daniel 7:1 – 8
I considered the horns, and behold, there came up among them another little horn, before whom there were 3 of the first horns plucked up by the roots: and, behold, in this horn were eyes like the eyes of man, and a moth speaking great things, Daniel 7:8.

Daniel's Visions are Explained, Daniel 7:20 – 28
And of the 10 horns that were in his head, and of the other which came up, and before whom 3 fell; even of that horn that had eyes, and a mouth that spake very great things, whose look was more stout than his fellows, Daniel 7:20.

Daniel's 2nd Vision: A Ram and a Goat, Daniel 8:1 – 14
Then I lifted up mine eyes, and saw, and, behold, there stood before the river a ram which had 2 horns: and the 2 horns were high; but one was higher than the other, and the higher came up last, Daniel 8:3.

And as I was considering, behold, an he goat came from the west on the face of the whole earth, and touched not the ground: and the goat had a notable horn between his eyes, Daniel 8:5.

<u>The Angel Gabriel Explains the Vision</u>, Daniel 8:15 – 27
And the rough goat is the king of Grecia: and the great horn that is between his eyes is the first king, Daniel 8:21.

<u>Daniel Prays for His People</u>, Daniel 9:1 – 19
O my God, incline thine ear, and hear; open thine eyes, and behold our desolations, and the city which is called by thy name: for we do not present out supplications before thee for our righteousnesses, but for thy great mercies, Daniel 9:18.

<u>Daniel's Vision of a Man</u>, Daniel 10:1 – 9
Then I lifted up mine eyes, and looked, and behold a certain man clothed in linen, whose loins were girded with fine gold of Uphaz, Daniel 10:5.

His body also was like the beryl, and his face as the appearance of lightning, and his eyes as lamps of fire, and his arms and his feet like in colour to polished brass, and the voice of his words like the voice of a multitude, Daniel 10:6.

CHAPTER 17

THE MINOR PROPHET BOOKS

Hosea, Joel, Amos, <u>Obadiah</u>, <u>Jonah</u>, Micah, <u>Nahum</u>, Habakkuk, Zephaniah, Haggai, Zechariah, and Malachi are the Minor Prophet Books in the Bible. The books of Obadiah, Jonah, and Nahum the word "eyes" is not mentioned.

The 12 books of the Minor Prophets consist of a total of 67 chapters. The longest books of the Minor Prophets are Hosea and Zechariah, which both have 14 chapters; the shortest book of the Minor Prophets is Obadiah with only one chapter.

The Book of Hosea

The Book of Hosea is the first of the 12 Minor Prophet Books. The Prophet Hosea lived in the northern kingdom between 755 and 725 BC. The book denounces the worship of other gods, other than the God of Israel. The 14 chapters of Hosea speaks on his marriage to an unfaithful wife named Gomer, which is referring to the unfaithful Israelites. The word "eyes" are mentioned once.

Note of Interests: Hosea was the last of the prophets of the northern kingdom. When the Assyrians/Babylonians invaded the north, someone escaped to the south and brought the manuscript of Hosea to the city of Jerusalem.

<u>The LORD's Anger Against Israel</u>, Hosea 13:1 – 16
I will ransom them from the power of the grave; I will redeem them from death: O death, I will be thy plagues; O grace, I will be thy destruction: repentance shall be hid from mine eyes, Hosea 13:14 KJV.

The Book of Joel

The Book of Joel has 3 chapters; it was written between 835 and 800 BC. His name means "Jehovah is God." Joel was trying to encourage the people to repent of their sins so that they could be brought back into right standing with God. The Prophet Joel, the son of Pethuel, prophesied and preached to the people of Judah. Judah is devasted by a vast swarm of locusts that destroys the fields of grain, the vineyards, the gardens, and the trees. This devastation came against Judah because of her sins. The word "eyes" is mentioned once.

<u>An Invasion of Locusts</u>, Joel 1:1 – 20
Is not the meat cut off before our eyes, yea, joy and gladness from the house of our God, Joel 1:16 KJV?

The Book of Amos

The Book of Amos has 9 chapters, 145 verses with 4,217 words. It was written around 755 BC. The Prophet Amos lived in the kingdom of Judah but preached in the northern kingdom of Israel. The Bible describes him as a "shepherd" and a "dresser of sycamore trees." Amos denounces the crimes against humanity and preached on social injustice in Israel. The word "eyes" is mentioned twice in the same chapter.

Note of Interests: Amos wasn't born into a priestly family, didn't come from the Levi tribe, wasn't trained to be a preacher, nor attend any of the prophetic schools in Jerusalem, but God called him to preach and prophesied to the rebellious Northern Kingdom of Israel, Amos 7:15.

<u>A Vision of the LORD at the Altar</u>, Amos 9:1 – 10
And though they go into captivity before their enemies, thence will I command the sword, and it shall slay them: and I will set mine eyes upon them for evil, and not for good, Amos 9:4 ASV.

Behold, the eyes of the LORD Jehovah are upon the sinful kingdom, and I will destroy it from off the face of the earth; save that I will not utterly destroy the house of Jacob, saith Jehovah, Amos 9:8 ASV.

The Book of Obadiah

The Book of Obadiah has 1 chapter with 21 verses. It is a prophecy against the nation Edom. The Edomites were descended from Jacob's brother Esau. Obadiah announces Edom's downfall to Babylon because Esau's nation refused to help Israel in their need.

The Book of Jonah

The Book of Jonah has 4 chapters. It tells of the Prophet Jonah, who was sent to Nineveh by God to prophesy their destruction, but he tries to escape his divine mission; but he couldn't. Once Nineveh repented, God did not destroy the people of Nineveh.

The Book of Micah

The Book of Micah has 7 chapters, and the word "eyes" is mentioned once. The Prophet Micah wrote it between 742 – 686 BC. He lived in a small village named Moresheth Gath, which was about 25 miles southwest of Jerusalem. The Prophet Micah addresses the unjust leaders, rulers, and priests of Israel. He defended the rights of the poor against the rich and powerful. The name Micah means, "Who is like God?" Micah also prophesied the deliverance of Israel from Babylon, and they would be re-established in Jerusalem.

The Nation Turns to the LORD, Micah 7:8 – 10
And mine enemy shall see [it], and shame shall cover her which said unto me, Where is Jehovah thy God? Mine eyes shall behold her; now shall she be trodden down as, the mire of the streets, Micah 7:10 Darby.

The Book of Nahum

The Book of Nahum is the 7th book of the 12 Minor Prophet Books with 3 chapters. The Prophet Nahum wrote it just before the fall of Nineveh in 612 BC. Nahum was sent by God to preach judgment to Nineveh for the 2nd time. Jonah was the 1st to preach to Nineveh about 120 years earlier. At that time, Nineveh repented, and God didn't destroy them.

The Book of Habakkuk

The Book of Habakkuk has 3 chapters, and it's a dialogue between the Prophet Habakkuk and God. Habakkuk asked God, how can He remain silent when the wicked prosper or allow iniquity to go unpunished. God told Habakkuk that Babylon would be His chastening rod against Judah because of their continue sinfulness. The Prophet Habakkuk wrote the Book Habakkuk between 612 and 589 BC, just before the fall of Judah. The name "Habakkuk" means "one who embraces." The word "eyes" is mentioned only once.

Habakkuk Complains to the LORD, Habakkuk 1:12 – 17
Thy eyes are too pure to behold evil, and thou canst not look on iniquity. Why lookest thou upon them that do unjust things, and holdest thy peace when the wicked devoureth the man that is more just than himself, Habakkuk 1:13 DRA?

The Book of Zephaniah

The Book of Zephaniah has 3 chapters. Zephaniah was the great - great grandson of Hezekiah, the King of Judah. The Book of Zephaniah is a message of judgment and encouragement. God is sovereign over all nations, the wicked will be punished, the righteous will be vindicated on judgment day, and God will bless those who repent and put their trust in Him. The word "eyes" are mentioned once.

Israel's Joy and Restoration, Zephaniah 3:14 – 20
At that time will I bring you in, and at that time will I gather you; for I will give you honor and praise among all the peoples of the earth, when I restore your fortunes before your eyes, says Yahweh, Zephaniah 3:20 WEB.

The Book of Haggai

The Book of Haggai has 2 chapters and 38 verses. The Prophet Haggai gave 4 messages to the Jews in Jerusalem. They had returned from exile in Babylon and been back 18 years but hadn't rebuilt the temple. These messages encouraged the Jews to finish building the temple and to put their hope in God. The word "eyes" is mentioned once in Haggai.

The LORD Encourages the People through Zerubbabel, Haggai 2:1 – 9
Who is left among you who saw this house in its former glory? How do you see it now? Isn't it in your eyes as nothing, Haggai 2:3 WEB?

The Book of Zephaniah

The Book of Zechariah has 14 chapters. The Prophet Zechariah was younger than Haggai, and he continued the ministry that Haggai began. Haggai chastised the people for their failure to rebuild the temple, but Zechariah encouraged the people to rebuild the temple by presenting to them the coming glory of the LORD. Zechariah had 8-night visions that brought the hope of the promised messianic kingdom, and challenge Israel after the exile to remain faithful to the LORD. In the Book of Zechariah, the word "eyes" is mentioned 14 times in 13 verses.

A Vision of Horns and Craftsmen, Zechariah 1:18 – 21
And I lifted up mine eyes, and saw, and, behold, 4 horns, Zechariah 1:18 ASV.

<u>A Vision of a Man with a Measuring Line</u>, Zechariah 2:1 – 13
And I lifted up mine eyes, and saw, and, behold, a man with a measuring line in his hand, Zechariah 2:1 ASV.

<u>A Vision of Joshua the High Priest</u>, Zechariah 3:1 – 10
For behold the stone that I have laid before Joshua; upon one stone shall be 7 eyes: behold, I will engrave the graving thereof, saith the LORD of hosts, and I will remove the iniquity of that land in one day, Zechariah 3:9 KJV.

<u>A Vision of a Golden Lampstand</u>, Zechariah 4:1 – 14
For who hath despised the day of small things? For they shall rejoice, and shall see the plummet in the hand of Zerubbabel with those 7; they are the eyes of the LORD, which run to and from through the whole earth, Zechariah 4:10 KJV.

<u>A Vision of a Flying Scroll</u>, Zechariah 5:1 – 4
Then again I lifted up mine eyes, and saw, and, behold, a flying roll, Zechariah 5:1 ASV.

<u>A Vision of a Woman in a Basket</u>, Zechariah 5:5 – 11
Then the angel that talked with me went forth, and said unto me, Lift up now thine eyes, and see what is this that goeth forth, Zechariah 5:5 ASV.

Then lifted I up mine eyes, and saw, and behold, there came forth 2 women, and the wind was in their wings; now they had wings like the wings of a stork; and they lifted up the ephah between the earth and the heaven, Zechariah 5:9 ASV.

A Vision of Four Chariots, Zechariah 6:1 – 8
And I lifted up mine eyes again, and saw, and behold, there came 4 chariots out from between 2 mountains; and the mountains were mountains of brass, Zechariah 6:1 Darby.

The Holy City of Peace and Prosperity, Zechariah 8:1 – 17
Thus saith Jehovah of hosts: If it be wonderful in the eyes of the remnant of this people in those days, should it also be wonderful in mine eyes? saith Jehovah of hosts, Zechariah 8:6 Darby.

Israel's Enemies Will Be Punished, Zechariah 9:1 – 8
The burden of the word of the LORD in the land of Hadrach, and Damascus shall be the rest thereof: when the eyes of man, as of all the tribes of Israel, shall be toward the LORD, Zechariah 9:1 KJV.

And I will encamp about mine house because of the army, because of him that passeth by, and because of him that returned: and no oppressor shall pass through them any more: for now have I seen with mine eyes, Zechariah 9:8 KJV.

The LORD Will Deliver Jerusalem, Zechariah 12:1 – 10
In that day, saith the LORD, I will strike every horse with astonishment, and his rider with madness: and I will open my eyes upon the house of Juda, and will strike every horse of the nations with blindness, Zechariah 12:4 DRA.

God's Judgment on Jerusalem's Attackers, Zechariah 14:12 – 15
And this shall be the plague wherewith the LORD shall strike all nations that have fought against Jerusalem: their flesh of every one shall consume away while they stand

upon their feet, and their eyes shall consume away in their holes, and their tongue shall consume away in their mouth, Zechariah 14:12 DRA.

The Book of Malachi

Malachi is the last book of the 12 Minor Prophet Books. Malachi was a Prophet of God sent to the Jews who had resettled in Judea, from their captivity in Babylon. The message of Malachi to the people was that the Great King would come not only to judge his people but also to bless and restore them, Malachi 4:2 – 4. The Book of Malachi has 4 chapters, and the word "eyes" is mentioned only in the 1st chapter.

The Lord's Love for Israel, Malachi 1:1 – 5
And your eyes shall see, and ye shall say, The LORD will be magnified from the border of Israel, Malachi 1:5 KJV.

CHAPTER 18

THE SYNOPTIC GOSPELS

The Gospel of Matthew is the first book of the New Testament. It is also the first book of the Synoptic Gospels, which include many of the same biblical events, incidents, and stories. The Synoptic Gospels are often written in a similar manner, sequence, and sometimes identical wording. The Gospels of Matthew, Mark, and Luke are referred to as the Synoptic Gospels.

The Gospel of Matthew tells how the promised Messiah was conceived, born, his ministry on earth, rejected by Israel, crucified, raised from the dead, and Jesus commission his disciples to preach the gospel to the whole world. Most scholars believe it was written between 80 and 90 AD, and others believe it was written between 70 – 110 AD.

Matthew was also known as "Levi." He was hated and despised by his own Jewish people because he was a tax collector, working for the Roman government. Jewish tax collectors were also called "publican." Most tax collectors became rich by collecting taxes from people, oftentimes, being dishonest by collecting an excessive amount of money. When Jesus called Matthew, he left his tax collection booth immediately to follow him, Matthew 9:9.

Note of Interests: Matthew's details regarding his call to follow Jesus is given in Mark and Luke's gospel; Mark 2:13 – 17 and Luke 5:27 – 32. It provides basically the same detail accounts as Matthew 9:9 – 13.

In the Gospel of Matthew, the word "eyes" is mentioned in 10 verses, and they are listed below in the King James Version with a subject title. The word "eyes" is mentioned in 6 verses in Mark, and 9 verses in Luke.

The Gospel of Matthew

<u>Jesus Heals 2 Blind Men</u>, Matthew 9:27 – 31
Then touched he their eyes, saying, According to your faith be it unto you, Matthew 9:29.

And their eyes were opened; and Jesus straitly charged them, saying, See that no man know it, Matthew 9:30.

<u>Disciples Asked Jesus Why He Speaks in Parables</u>,
Matthew 13:10 – 17
For this people's heart is waxed gross, and their ears are dull of hearing, and their eyes they have closed; lest at any time they should see with their eyes and hear with their ears, and should understand with their heart, and should be converted, and I should heal them, Matthew 13:15.

But blessed are your eyes, for they see: and your ears, for they hear, Matthew 13:16.

<u>Jesus' Transfiguration</u>, Matthew 17:1 – 13
And when they had lifted up their eyes, they saw no man, save Jesus only, Matthew 17:8.

<u>Temptations to Sin</u>, Matthew 18:6 – 9
And if thine eye offend thee, pluck it out, and cast it from thee: it is better for thee to enter into life with one eye, rather than having 2 eyes to be cast into hell fire, Matthew 18:9.

<u>Two Blind Men Sitting by the Roadside Receive Sight</u>,
Matthew 20:29 – 34
They say unto him, LORD, that our eyes may be opened,
Matthew 20:33.

So, Jesus had compassion on them, and touched their eyes:
and immediately their eyes received sight, and they followed
him, Matthew 20:34.

<u>Jesus' Parable of the Tenants</u>, Matthew 21:33 – 46
Jesus saith unto them, Did ye never read in the scriptures,
The stone which the builders rejected, the same is become
the head of the corner: this is the LORD's doing, and it is
marvellous in our eyes, Matthew 21:42?

<u>A Place Called Gethsemane</u>, Matthew 26:36 – 46
And he came and found them asleep again: for their eyes
were heavy, Matthew 26:43.

The Gospel of Mark

The Gospel of Mark is the shortest book of the 4 gospels
with 16 chapters. Mark presents the Lord Jesus as the
Messiah, the Son of God who was sent to suffer, serve,
rescue, and restore mankind. It records the events of the
adult life and teachings of Jesus.

Mark the Evangelist was defined as John Mark, traditionally
in the Bible. He was Barnabas' cousin, a helper on Paul first
missionary journey, even though he did not stay for the
entire trip. John Mark was also a companion of Simon Peter
and assisted him in Rome. The verses from the Gospel of
Mark, in which the word "eyes" is mentioned comes from
the World English Bible.

<u>Yeast of the Pharisees and Herod</u>, Mark 8:14 – 21
Having eyes, don't you see? Having ears, don't you hear?
Don't not remember, Mark 8:18?

<u>Jesus Heals a Blind Man at Bethsaida</u>, Mark 8:22 – 26
He took hold of the blind man by the hand, and brought him
out of the village. When he had spit on his eyes, and laid his
hands on him, he asked him if he saw anything, Mark 8:23.

Then again he laid his hands on his eyes. He looked intently,
and was restored, and saw everyone clearly, Mark 8:25.

<u>Leading People to Sin</u>, Mark 9:42 – 50
If your eye causes you to stumble, cast it out. It is better for
you to enter into God's Kingdom with one eye, rather than
having two eyes to be cast into Gehenna fire, Mark 9:47.

<u>Jesus' Parable of the Wicked Vinedressers</u>, Mark 12:1 – 12
This was from the LORD, it is marvelous in our eyes,
Mark 12:11?

<u>Jesus' Prayer in the Garden Named Gethsemane</u>,
Mark 14:32 – 42
Again he returned, and found them sleeping, for their eyes
were very heavy, and they didn't know what to answer him,
Mark 14:40.

The Gospel of Luke

The Gospel of Luke tells of Jesus Christ origins, birth,
ministry, death, resurrection, and ascension. He is the only
Gentile Christian writer of the New Testament. Luke was
a Greek physician and close companion of the Apostle Paul.
He was not one of the 12 Apostles. However, he spelled

out his purpose for writing his gospel in the 1st 4 verses of chapter 1 of Luke. The objective was to give a reliable and precise historical record of the life of Jesus Christ.

The Gospel of Luke contains the most verses and words than any other book in the New Testament, even though it has only 24 chapters compared to Matthew and Acts with 28 chapters. It was written between 58 and 65 AD. The 9 verses that contain the word "eyes" is from the American Standard Version.

<u>Simeon Sees Jesus in the Temple</u>, Luke 2:25 – 35
For mine eyes have seen thy salvation, Luke 2:30.

<u>Jesus is Rejected at Nazareth</u>, Luke 4:14 – 30
And he closed the book, and gave it back to the attendant, and say down: and the eyes of all in the synagogue were fastened on him, Luke 4:20.

<u>The Beatitudes</u>, Luke 6:20 – 22
And he lifted up his eyes on his disciples, and said, Blessed be ye poor: for yours is the kingdom of God, Luke 6:20.

<u>Jesus Prays to the Father</u>, Luke 10:21 – 24
And turning to the disciples, he said privately, Blessed are the eyes which see the things that ye see, Luke 10:23.

<u>The Rich Man and Lazarus</u>, Luke 16:19 – 31
And in Hades he lift up his eyes, being in torments, and seeth Abraham afar off, and Lazarus in his bosom, Luke 16:23.

<u>The Pharisee and the Publican</u>, Luke 18:9 – 14
But the publican, standing afar off, would not lift up so much as his eyes unto heaven, but smote upon his breast, saying, God be thou merciful to me a sinner, Luke 18:13.

<u>Jesus Weeps Over Jerusalem</u>, Luke 19:41 – 44
Saying, If thou hadst known in this day, even thou, the things which belong unto peace! but now they are hid from thine eyes, Luke 19:42.

<u>Jesus Appears on the Road to Emmaus</u>, Luke 24:13 – 35
But their eyes were holden that they should not know him, Luke 24:16.

And their eyes were opened, and they knew him; and he vanished out of their sight, Luke 24:31.

CHAPTER 19

ACTS OF THE APOSTLES

Luke the Apostle wrote the Book of Acts, which is also called the Acts of the Apostles. He also wrote the Gospel of Luke, which tells how God fulfilled his plan for the world's salvation through Jesus' life, death, and resurrection; the promised Messiah. The Book of Acts continues the events surrounding salvation and Christianity in the 1st century, beginning with Jesus' ascension to heaven, Acts 1:1 – 11.

The Book of Acts has 28 chapters, which chronicles the history of the founding and spread of the early Christian Churches from Jerusalem to Rome. A brief outline is given below.

I. The Early Spread of the Church in Jerusalem, Acts 1:1 – Acts 7:60

  1. Jesus Ascends to Heaven, Acts 1:1 – 11
  2. Matthias is chosen to replace Judas, Acts 1:12 – 26
  3. The Holy Spirit comes upon the Apostles on Pentecost, Acts 1
  4. Peter Preaches, Jesus they Crucified, Acts 2:14 - 36
  5. The Church Begins, Acts 2:37 – 47
  6. Persecution Begins, Acts 3:1 – Acts 4:31
  7. The Believers Share with Each Other, Acts 4:32 – 37
  8. Ananias and Sapphira are Slain for Lying to God, Acts 5:1 – 11
  9. A Second Wave of Persecution Erupts, Acts 5:12 – 42

10. Provision is made for Neglected Grecian Widows, Acts 6:1 – 7
11. Stephen is Arrested, Acts 6:8 – 15
12. Stephen Speech about Abraham's Call, Acts 7:1 – 53
13. Stephen is Stoned to Death, Acts 7:54 – 60

II. The Church Spreads to Samaria, Acts 8:1 – 9:31

1. Increased Persecution and the Church Scatters throughout Judea and Samaria, Acts 8:1 – 4
2. Philip Preaches in Samaria, Acts 8:5 – 8
3. Simon the Sorcerer is Converted, Acts 8:9 – 25
4. Philip Teaches an Ethiopian, Acts 8:26 – 40
5. The Account of Saul's Conversion, Acts 9:1 – 31

III. The Church Spreads to Phoenicia, Cyprus, and Antioch, Acts 9:32 – Acts 12:25

1. Peter Raises Dorcas from the Dead, Acts 9:32 – 43
2. Peter to take the Gospel to the Gentile Cornelius, Acts 10:1 – 48
3. Peter explains his actions to the Jewish Christians in Judea, Acts 11:1 – 18
4. A Gentile Church Starts in Antioch, Acts 11:19 – 30
5. Peter is Imprisoned by Herod and Released by God, Acts 12:1 – 19
6. Herod Dies, Acts 12:20 – 25

IV. The Extension of the Church from Antioch to Galatia, Acts 13:1 – Acts 15:35

1. Paul take His First Missionary Journey, Acts 13:1 – Acts 14:28

2. A Council is Held in Jerusalem to Determine Behavior for Gentile Christians, Acts 15:1 – 35

V. The Extension of the Church to Macedonia, Acts 15:36 – Acts 21:16

1. Paul's Second Missionary Journey is Recorded, Acts 15:36 – Acts 18:22
2. Paul's Third Missionary Journey is Recorded, Acts 18:23 – Acts 21:16

VI. The Years of Paul's Imprisonment, Acts 21:17 – Acts 28:31

1. Paul in Jerusalem, Acts 21:17 – Acts 23:35
2. Paul in Caesarea, Acts 24:1 – Acts 26:32
3. Paul's Voyage to Rome, Acts 27:1 – Acts 28:15
4. Paul in Rome, Acts 28:16 – 31

The Book of Acts and the Gospel of Luke are unique because they are addressed to "Theophilus." The name "Theophilus" means "friend of God."

Note of Interests: The name "Theophilus" is also written "Theophilos," in English. The name "Theophilus" means "loved by God," as well as a "friend of God." Some scholars believe that "Theophilus" is just a generic title that applies to all Christians.

The name "Theophilus" was an honorary title among the educated Romans and Jews. Many scholars believe that Luke wrote to a Jewish high priest named Theophilus ben Ananus. Theophilus ben Anaus was a high priest in

Jerusalem around 37 AD. He was the son of Annas and the brother-in-law of Caiaphas.

Others scholar believes that Luke wrote to a specific individual because of the title "most excellent Theophilus," Luke 1:3. The title "most excellent" is used when referring to an individual with honor or rank, such as a Roman official. Apostle Paul used the same term when he was addressed Felix and Festus, Acts 23:26, Acts 24:2, and Acts 26:25.

Others suggest that Theophilus was a wealthy man in the city of Antioch. There are references to a man named Theophilus, who was a great leader in the city of Antioch during the time of Luke. Scholars believe, he could have been a financial supporter of Paul and Luke on their missionary journeys; this would explain why Luke provides an orderly and detailed account of what had happened.

Other scholars believe that Theophilus was a high priest named Mattathias ben Theophilus, who served in Jerusalem around 65 AD. Still, others think that Theophilus was the Roman lawyer who defended Paul during his trial in Rome. They believe that Luke's purpose in writing Luke and Acts was to write a legal defense; like a legal brief. On this belief, Luke's writings were designed to defend Paul in court against the charge of rebellion and defend Christianity against the charge that it was an anti-Roman religion.

The word "eyes" is mentioned in the Acts of the Apostles 9 times in 8 verses; twice in Acts 28:27. They are listed below from the Douay-Rheims 1899 American Edition with a subject title.

<u>Peter and John Heals a Crippled Man</u>, Acts 3:1 - 26
But Peter with John fastening his eyes upon him, said: Look upon us, Acts 3:4.

<u>Saul Encounters with the Risen Jesus</u>, Acts 9:1 – 18
And Saul arose from the ground; and when his eyes were opened, he saw nothing. But they leading him by the hands, brought him to Damascus, Acts 9:8.

And immediately there fell from his eyes as it were scales, and he received sight his sight; and rising up, he was baptized, Acts 9:18.

<u>Peter Restored Dorcas to Life</u>, Acts 9:36 – 43
And they all being put forth, Peter kneeling down prayed, and turning to the body, he said: Tabitha, arise. And she opened her eyes; and seeing Peter, she sat up, Acts 9:40.

Note of Interests: The lady named Dorcas in the Book of Acts is also called Tabitha. She was a disciple of Jesus and lived in Joppa, a city on the coast of the Mediterranean Sea. The name "Dorcas" is a Greek name which means "gazelle," and the name "Tabitha" is Aramaic. Dorcas was a charitable lady who made clothes for the needy in Joppa. Dorcas dies, and her fellow disciples called for Peter, who was in the neighboring city of Lydda, and he raised her from the dead. The city Lydda was about 11 miles SE of Joppa.

Peter's Vision, Acts 11:1 – 18
Into which looking, I considered, and saw fourfooted creatures of the earth, and beasts, and creeping things, and fowls of the air, Acts 11:6. **PS:** Douay-Rheims 1899 American Edition (DRA) doesn't used the word "eyes" in Acts 11:6; King James Version reads: Upon the which when I had fastened mine eyes, I considered, and saw four-footed beasts of the earth, and wild beasts, and creeping things, and fowls of the air, Acts 11:6.

Paul's 1st Missionary Journey, Acts 13:4 – 12
Then Saul, otherwise Paul, filled with the Holy Ghost looking upon him, Acts 13:9. **PS:** Douay-Rheims 1899 American Edition (DRA) doesn't used the word "eyes" in Acts 13:9; King James Version reads: Then Saul, (who also is called Paul,) filled with the Holy Ghost, set his eyes on him, Acts 13:9.

Notes of Interests: Luke speaks about himself being part of the 2nd missionary journey in Troas and Macedonia, Acts 16:10 – 17. Luke was also present on the journey back from Macedonia to Jerusalem, Acts 20:5 – 21:18. Luke is also on the journey to Rome from Caesarea, Acts 27:1 – 28:16.

Paul Speaks of His Conversion, Acts 26:12 – 18
To open their eyes, that they may be concerted from darkness to light, and from the power of Satan to God, that they may receive forgiveness of sins, and a lot among the saints, by the faith that is in me, Acts 26:18.

Paul in Rome, Acts 28:16 – 31

For the heart of this people is grown gross, and their ears have they heard heavily, and their eyes they have shut; lest perhaps they should see with their eyes, and hear with their ears, and understand with their hearts, and should be converted, and I should heal them, Acts 28:27.

The Book of Acts covers approximately 30 years of church history. Acts begin with the ascension of Christ and run through to 62 – 64 AD. The Book of Acts speaks on the event surrounding the first Christian martyr, named Stephen. Acts reveal the conversion of Saul of Damascus to Paul and mention the 3 Pauline mission trips.

CHAPTER 20
THE EPISTLES OF PAUL

Biblical scholars do not agree on the number of epistles that Paul wrote. There is little dispute that Paul wrote Romans, 1 Corinthians, 2 Corinthians, Galatians, Philippians, 1 Thessalonians, and Philemon; 7 epistles.

However, 14 epistles have been attributed to Paul. They are **Romans, 1 Corinthians, 2 Corinthians, Galatians,** Ephesians, **Philippians,** Colossians, **1 Thessalonians, 2 Thessalonians,** Hebrews, 1 Timothy, 2 Timothy, Titus, and **Philemon.** The 4 Epistles of Apostle Paul that contain the word "eyes" are listed below with a subject title.

Note of Interests: An epistle is a formal writing directed or sent to an individual, or group of people. It is an elegantly written letter which usually conveys instructions and information. The epistle style of letter-writing was common in Ancient Egypt as part of the scribal-school writing curriculum. It begins with several statements introducing the main topic of the entire letter. The letters in the New Testament that were from Apostles to Christians are usually referred to as epistles. The epistles traditionally credited to Paul are known as Pauline epistles. The other epistles in the New Testament are called general epistles which are Epistle of James, First Epistle of Peter, Second Epistle of Peter, First Epistle of John, Second Epistle of John, Third Epistle of John, and the Epistle of Jude.

The Epistles to the Romans

The Epistle to the Romans is often called Romans. It is the 6th book in the New Testament with 16 chapters. Paul wrote it from Corinth on his 3rd missionary journey. Scholars believe it was written around 60 AD. Paul speaks on the prayer of thanksgiving, righteousness of God, condemnation, justification, explains that salvation is offered through the gospel of Jesus Christ. The Epistle of Paul to the Romans is the longest of the Pauline Epistles and the first letter of Paul in the Bible.

Note of Interests: Paul never traveled to Rome, but he longed to go. He sent this epistle ahead of him, as a way of introducing himself, Romans 1:10 – 12. In chapter 16 of Romans, Paul greets by name 27 people in a congregation he had never visited. The names are in the back of the book; *smile.*

Some scholars call the Book of Romans, Paul's greatest work. Others call Romans, "The Gospel, according to Paul." The Book of Romans explains in detail the great significance of Christ's sacrificial death on the cross. In the epistles to the Romans, the word "eyes" is mentioned in 3 verses.

<u>All People are Guilty</u>, Romans 3:9 – 20
There is no fear of God before their eyes, Romans 3:18 WEB.

Israel and God's Faithfulness, Romans 11:1 – 10
According as it is written, God has given to them a spirit of slumber, eyes not to see, and ears not to hear, unto this day, Romans 11:8 Darby.

Let their eyes be darkened not to see, and bow down their back always, Romans 11:10 Darby.

The Epistle to the Galatians

One of Paul, most significant letter was the Epistle to the Galatians, which is the 9th book in the New Testament with 6 chapters. It was a letter sent to several Christian communities in Galatia. The Epistle to the Galatians is a call for freedom from the law. The church in Galatia had abandoned the gospel they originally received from the Apostles. The Judaizers had infiltrated the brethren, preaching circumcision and placing them back under the yoke of the law. The word "eyes" appear in two verses in the epistle to the Galatians.

Note of Interests: Judaizers refer to Jewish Christians who sought to persuade Gentile Christians to observe Jewish religious customs. The Judaizers' doctrine was a mixture of grace through Christ and the keeping of the Law of Moses. This false doctrine was condemned in the epistle of Galatians.

By Faith or the Works of the Law, Galatians 3:1 – 14
O foolish Galatians, who did bewitch you, before whose eyes Jesus Christ was openly set forth crucified, Galatians 3:1 ASV?

<u>Paul's Concern for the Galatians</u>, Galatians 4:8 – 20

Where then is that gratulation of yourselves? for I bear you witness, that, if possible, ye would have plucked out your eyes and given them to me, Galatians 4:15 ASV.

The Epistle to the Ephesians

The Epistle to the Ephesians is also called Ephesians. It is the 10th book of the New Testament with 6 chapters. It was written while Paul was in prison at Rome, Ephesians 3:1, Ephesians 4:1.

Philippians, Ephesians, Colossians, and Philemon are known as Paul's Prison Epistles. They were written during the time Paul was under house arrest in Rome between 60 – 62 AD. The 4 Prison Epistle of Paul consists of 3 epistles written to the church of Ephesus, Colosse, and Philippi, and one personal epistle to his friend, Philemon.

Note of Interests: Philemon was a wealthy owner of a runaway servant named Onesimus. Onesimus had become a new believer in Christ Jesus, and minister to Paul in prison. Paul's epistle pleas with Philemon to forgive Onesimus and treat him like a brother in Christ. Paul offered to pay Onesimus' debt to his master.

The purpose of the Epistle to the Ephesians was to warn the church elders about false teachers that were teaching a false gospel. In the epistles to the Ephesians, the word "eyes" is mentioned once.

Paul's Prayer, Ephesians 1:15 - 23
The eyes of your understanding being enlightened; that ye may know what is the hope of his calling, and what the riches of the glory of his inheritance in the saints, Ephesians 1:18 KJV.

The Epistle to the Hebrews

The Epistle to the Hebrews begins by saying that Jesus is the final revelation from God spoken about in the Old Testament, Hebrews 1:1 – 4. The LORD Jesus Christ is superior in comparison to Judaism and the old covenant.

The Epistle of Hebrews teaches that Jesus took away our sins by dying on the cross, therefore, we should now draw near to God with confidence, and know that we are justified. The Epistle to the Hebrews encourages wavering Jewish Christians to remain loyal to Jesus. It stresses the absolute supremacy, sufficiency, and superiority of Jesus Christ.

Note of Interests: While researching, I discovered Hebrews, chapter 11 is considered one of the 10 most popular chapters in the Bible. They are listed below with a subject title.

1. Genesis 1 – The Creation Account
2. Genesis 37 – Joseph and the Coat of many Colors
3. Exodus 20 – The Ten Commandments
4. Daniel 3 – Shadrach, Meschach, and Abednego
5. Daniel 6 – Daniel and the Lion's Den
6. Matthew 28 – The Resurrection of Jesus
7. Luke 2 – The Birth of Jesus the Christ
8. John 1 – The Word
9. Hebrews 11 – The Hall of Faith
10. Acts 9 – The Conversion of Saul

The Epistle to the Hebrews is considered a General Epistle written around 67 AD. It has 13 chapters with the word "eyes" mentioned in only chapter 4 of Hebrews.

<u>The Enter the Promised Rest</u>, Hebrews 4:1 – 16
Neither is there any creature invisible in his sight: but all things are naked and opened to his eyes, to whom our speech is, Hebrews 4:13 DRA.

Question: Which Epistles of Paul doesn't contain the word "eyes?"
Father God had to throw at least one Question and Answer moment in the book for you. Smile and Praise Him.

1. _____
2. _____
3. _____
4. _____
5. _____
6. _____
7. _____
8. _____
9. _____
10. _____

Answer in the back of the book

CHAPTER 21

THE LEADER OF THE EARLY CHURCH

The name "Peter" in English means "a rock," and it is derived from the Greek word "Petros," which means "stone, rock, petra." Peter in the Bible was a fisherman and later became a disciple and Apostle of Jesus. He had an impulsive nature, but rock-like faith in Jesus.

Peter was originally from Bethsaida but lived in Capernaum. Bethsaida and Capernaum were both located on the coast of the Sea of Galilee. Peter, James, and John were partners in the fishing industry. Jesus called Peter to follow Him, after producing a miraculous catch of fish for them, Luke 5:1 – 7. Peter immediately left everything behind to follow Jesus, and the next 3 years lived as a disciple of the LORD Jesus, Luke 5:11.

Note of Interests: Bethsaida was known as a fishing village. The name means "house of fishing;" it was approximately 3 miles east of Capernaum.

Peter was one of the 12 Apostle of Jesus Christ. He is also known as Simon Peter, Simeon, Simon, Cephas, and Apostle Peter. Peter was a fisherman in Bethsaida, along with his brother Andrew, when Jesus called them to be "fishers of men," Matthew 4:18 – 19.

Note of Interests: The names of Jesus first 12 Apostles were Simon who is called Peter, his brother Andrew; James son of Zebedee, and his brother John; Philip, Bartholomew, Thomas, Matthew the tax collector; James the son of Alphaeus; Thaddaeus, Simon the Zealot; and Judas Iscariot, who betrayed him, Matthew 10:2 – 4. The word "Apostle" means "one who is sent" or "one who is commissioned" to do a task. The word Apostle appears 18 times in the KJV New Testament, only. In Hebrews 3:1 – 2, the word was applied to Jesus, who was sent by God. It reads, "Wherefore, holy brethren, partakers of a heavenly calling, consider the Apostle and High Priest of our confession, even Jesus; who was faithful to him that appointed him, as also was Moses in all his house," ASV.

Peter was also one of Jesus' closest disciple, along with James and John. He was the 1st disciple called by Jesus, and 1st Apostle commissioned by Him. The Gospel books and Acts of the Disciples portray Peter as the most prominent Apostle, even though he denied Jesus 3 times during the events of the crucifixion. Many times, Peter confesses his faith in Jesus as the Messiah.

Note of Interests: Peter was the 1st of the disciples to confess Jesus as "the Christ, the Son of the living God," a truth which Jesus said was divinely revealed to Peter, Matthew 16:16 – 17.

Many scholars believe that Peter had an authority that superseded that of the other Apostles. He was the Apostles spokesman at several events in the Bible. Peter conducted the election of Matthias, and his opinion in the debate over converting Gentiles was crucial.

The Synoptic Gospels mention how Jesus healed Peter's mother-in-law at their home in Capernaum, Matthew 8, Mark 1, and Luke 4. In Luke's gospel, Peter owns the boat that Jesus uses to preach to the multitudes at the shore of Lake Gennesaret, Luke 5. Jesus then amazes Simon Peter, and his companions James and John by telling them to lower their nets, at which point they catch a vast number of fishes. Immediately after this, they became a disciple of Jesus and followed him, Luke 5.

The Gospel of Matthew, Mark, and John mention the story of Jesus walking on water, but Matthew's gospel describes Peter walking on water for a moment but begins to sink when his faith wavers, Matthew 14:28 – 31.

At the Last Supper, Jesus washed his disciples' feet. Peter initially refused to allow Jesus to wash his feet, but when Jesus responded, "If I wash thee not, thou hast no part with me." Peter replied, "Lord, not my feet only, but also my hands and my head," John 13:2 – 11.

The Synoptic Gospels mention when Jesus was arrested, one of his disciples cut off the ear of a servant of the High Priest. The Gospel of John also includes this event, and names Peter as the swordsman, and Malchus as the victim, John 18:10. Luke's gospel stated that Jesus touched the ear and healed it, Luke 22:49 – 51.

Note of Interests: Jesus healing the servant's ear is the last healing miracle attributed to Jesus in the Bible. Apostle John wrote, "And there are also many other things which Jesus did, the which, if they should be written every one, I suppose that even the world itself could not contain the books that should be written; Amen," John 21:25. The 37 miracles of Jesus mentioned in the Bible are recorded in the back of the book for your blessedness.

Peter was arrested with John, twice, Acts 4:7 – 22 and Acts 5:17 – 42. According to Acts 10, Peter received a vision from God concerning the eating of previously unclean animals, and God told him to eat, twice. The unclean animals in the vision symbolized the Gentiles. God wanted Peter to take the gospel to the Gentiles, and he was instrumental in the decision to evangelize the Gentiles, Acts 10.

In the Book of Acts, Peter and John were sent from Jerusalem to Samaria, Acts 8:14. Peter also called Cephas is mentioned briefly in the opening chapter of Paul's Epistle to Galatians, Galatians 1:18. According to Acts 12, Peter was in Jerusalem when he was put in prison by King Herod but was rescued by an Angel. Afterward, Peter left Jerusalem, Acts 12:1 – 18.

Peter is recognized as the 1st leader of the early church. According to tradition, Peter was crucified in Rome under Emperor Nero around 65 A.D. The ancient Christian Churches all revere Peter as a great saint and the founder of the Church of Antioch and the Church of Rome. According to Catholic teaching, in Matthew 16:18, Jesus promised Peter a special position in the church.

And I say to thee:
That thou art Peter; and upon this
rock I will build my church,
and the gates of hell shall not prevail against it.
Matthew 16:18 DRA

The Catholic undoubtedly believes that Simon Peter was distinguished by Jesus to hold the 1st place of honor and authority. He was the 1st Bishop of Rome; the 1st Pope.

Apostle Peter wrote 2 brief epistles around 60 AD to Jesus' believers. They are known as 1st and 2nd Peter around 60 AD. 1st Peter has 5 chapters, and 2nd Peter has 3 chapters. These epistles encourage the believers to remain steadfast to the end that lived in the 5 provinces of Pontus, Galatia, Cappadocia, Asia, and Bithynia.

1st Peter encourages, strengthen, and comfort the persecuted and suffering believers of Jesus Christ. It explains the doctrines of Christianity and taught believers to be humble to others for the cause of Christ. 2nd Peter warned the believer of Jesus Christ concerning false teachers attacking the gospel of Jesus. It encouraged the believers to "grow in grace and knowledge." The 2nd Epistle of Peter also explained why the LORD's Second Coming was delayed, 2 Peter 3:1 – 13. The word "eyes" is mentioned once in each epistle, which is listed below.

The Epistle of 1st Peter

The Epistle of 1st Peter has 1684 words, 105 verses, and 5 chapters. It's the 60th book in the Bible. In 1st Peter, more than 1/3 of the 105 verses refers to the Old Testament. It was written around 64 AD from Babylon, 1 Peter 5:13. **PS:** 1/3 of 105 verses is 35 verses; I had to get the calculator out . . . *smile*

Blessing for Doing Right, 1 Peter 3:8 – 12
For the eyes of the LORD are upon the righteous, And his ears unto their supplication: But the face of the LORD is upon them that do evil, 1 Peter 3:12 ASV.

The Epistle of 2 Peter

The 2nd Epistle of Peter has 3 chapters with 1099 words, and 61 verses. Scholars believe that the 2nd Epistle of Peter was written about 67 AD, approximately 3 years after the 1st Epistle of Peter, and shortly before Peter's death, 2 Peter 1:14. The 2nd Epistle of Peter shares several unique words with the 1st Epistle of Peter, along with Peter's speeches in the Book of Acts. 1st and 2nd Peter, both mentions Noah and the flood, 1 Peter 3:20 and 2 Peter 2:5. The 2nd chapter of 2nd Peter warns against false prophets, teachers, and doctrine is similar to the Book of Jude warning that false teachers have slipped in among the believers. The Book of Jude has only 1 chapter with 25 verses.

Moral Wickedness of False Teachers, 2 Peter 2:12 – 18
Having eyes full of adultery, and that cannot cease from sin; enticing unstedfast souls; having a heart exercised in covetousness; children of cursing, 2 Peter 2:14 ASV.

Note of Interests: Other books beside 1st and 2nd Peter that bears Peter name are the Acts of Peter, Preaching of Peter, Apocalypse of Peter, and Judgement of Peter. These books are considered as apocryphal and are not included in the biblical canon. Apocryphal is writings by early Christians that give an account of Jesus' teaching, the nature of God, and the teachings of Jesus' Apostles. The word "Apocryphal" means "things put away" or "things hidden."

The Catholic Church recognizes Peter as the head of its church on earth with Christ being the heavenly head. A statue of Peter is in St. Peter's Square at the Vatican.

CHAPTER 22

JOHN THE APOSTLE

John, the son of Zebedee, was one of the 12 Apostles of Jesus. He was the youngest of the Apostles. John had a brother named James, and he was also one of the Apostles of Jesus Christ.

Note of Interests: Zebedee was the father of John and James, two of Jesus' disciples. Scholars believe he was the husband of Salome, one of the women present at the crucifixion. Zebedee was a fisherman, and his name is mentioned in the 4 gospels. In the gospel of Matthew and Mark, Zebedee was left in the boat after Jesus called his sons James and John to follow him, Matthew 4:21 – 22 and Mark 1:19 – 20. The Gospel of Mark, states that Zebedee was left with the "hired men," in the boat. The other 5 times Zebedee's name is mention is relating to the fact that James and John are his sons.

John the Apostle is identified as John the Evangelist, John of Patmos, John the Elder, and the Beloved Disciples by the Early Church Fathers. He outlived the other disciples and was the only Apostle of Jesus to die of natural causes.

Jesus referred to the brothers, James and John, as "Boanerges," which means "sons of thunder." Peter, James, and John were the only witness of the raising of the Daughter of Jairus from the dead. All three witnessed the Transfiguration of Jesus, and these same three witnessed the Agony in Gethsemane more closely than the other Apostles.

John reported to Jesus that they had forbidden a non-disciple from casting out demons in Jesus' name, prompting Jesus to say, "he who is not against us is on our side," Luke 1:49 – 50.

Jesus sent only John and Peter into the city to prepare for the final Passover meal, known as the Last Supper. At the meal itself, the disciple "whom Jesus loved" sat next to him which is believed to be John. When Jesus was arrested, John followed Jesus into the palace of the high priest.

Note of Interests: The words "whom Jesus loved" is mentioned 5 times only in the Gospel of John.

John remained near Jesus at the foot of the cross on Calvary. John took Mary, the mother of Jesus, into his care as the last legacy of Jesus, John 19:25 – 27.

After Jesus' Ascension and the descent of the Holy Spirit at Pentecost, John, together with Peter, took a prominent part in the founding and guidance of the church. Apostle John was with Peter with the healing of the lame man at Solomon Porch at the Temple, Acts 3:1 – 10. John was also thrown in prison with Peter, Acts 4. Apostle John went with Peter to visit the newly converted believers in Samaria, Acts 8:14.

Saint John wrote the Gospel of John and the Books of 1 John, 2 John, 3 John and Revelation. The word "eyes" is mentioned in the Gospel of John 17 times; 1st John only 3 times, and the Book of Revelation 9 times. The verses from the Gospel of John in which the word "eyes" is mentioned are listed below from KJV with a short introductory title.

The Gospel of John

The Samaritans, John 4:39 – 45
Say not ye, There are yet 4 months, and then cometh harvest? Behold, I say unto you, Lift up your eyes, and look on the fields; for they are white already to harvest, John 4:35.

Note of Interests: The Samaritans in Jesus' era began as a race of people in the Old Testament. The Samaritans occupied the territory which once belonged to the tribes of Ephraim and the half-tribe of Manasseh. The capital of this territory was called Samaria, the land which lies north of Judea and south of Galilee.

When the Northern Kingdom which consisted of 10 tribes were carried away into captivity to Assyria, according to 2 Kings 17:24, the king of Assyria sent people from Cutha, Ava, Hamath, and Sepharvaim to inhabit Samaria. They eventually intermarried with the Israelites that were still in Samaria. As a result, their children were considered only half-Jewish by the Jews. The Jews despised the Samaritans and wanted nothing to do with them.

The Jews and Samaritans believed that they came from the seed of Abraham, Isaac, and Jacob. They both considered Moses a prophet and the lawgiver from the LORD. The Samaritans embrace a religion mixed with Judaism and idolatry. The Samaritans center of worship was at Mount Gerizim, instead of Jerusalem.

Samaria eventually became a place of refuge for all the outlaws of Judea, Joshua 20:6 – 7. Despite the hatred between the Jews and the Samaritans, Jesus preached the gospel of peace to the Samaritans, John 4. The Apostles of Jesus also preached the Gospel of Jesus in Samaritan towns, Acts 8:25.

<u>Jesus Heals at Bethesda</u>, John 6:1 – 17
When Jesus then lifted up his eyes, and saw a great company come unto him, he saith unto Philip, Whence, shall we buy bread, that these may eat, John 6:5?

<u>Jesus Heals a Man Born Blind</u>, John 9:1 – 41
When he had thus spoken, he spat on the ground, and made clay of the spittle, and he anointed the eyes of the blind man with clay, John 9:6.

Therefore, said they unto him, How were thine eyes opened, John 9:10?

The answered and said, A man that is called Jesus made clay, and anointed mine eyes, and said unto me, Go to the pool of Siloam, and wash: and I went and washed, and I received sight, John 9:11.

And it was the sabbath day when Jesus made the clay and opened his eyes, John 9:14.

Then again, the Pharisees also asked him how he had received his sight. He said unto them, He put clay upon mine eyes, and I washed, and do see, John 9:15.

They say unto the blind man again, What sayest thou of him, that he hath opened thine eyes? He said, He is a prophet, John 9:17.

But by what means he now seeth, we know not; or who hath opened his eyes, we know not: he is of age; ask him: he shall speak for himself, John 9:21.

Then said they to him again, What did he to thee? How opened he thine eyes, John 9:26?

The man answered and said unto them, Why herein is a marvellous thing, that ye know not from whence he is, and yet he hath opened mine eyes, John 9:30.

Since the world began was it not heard that any many opened the eyes of one that was born blind, John 9:32.

I Am the Good Shepherd, John 10:1 – 21
Others said, These are not the words of him that hath a devil. Can a devil open the eyes of the blind, John 10:21?

The Death of Lazarus, John 11:1 – 44
And some of them said, Could not this man, which opened the eyes of the blind, have caused that even this man should not have died, John 11:37?

Then they took away the stone from the place where the dead was laid. And Jesus lifted up his eyes, and said, Father, I thank thee that thou hast heard me, John 11:41.

<u>The Belief and Unbelief Among the Jews</u>, John 12:37 – 50
He hath blinded their eyes and hardened their heart; that they should not see with their eyes, nor understand with their heart, and be converted, and I should heal them, John 12:40.

<u>Jesus Prays</u>, John 17:1 – 26
These words spake Jesus, and lifted up his eyes to heaven, and said, Father, the hour is come; glorify thy Son, that they Son also may glorify thee, John 17:1.

1 John 1

The First Epistle of John is the 23rd book of the New Testament, and the 62nd book of the Bible. The purpose of this epistle was to warn Believers about false teachings, assure them of their salvation, and remind them that Jesus Christ is the way, the truth, and the life. The 3 verses that contain the word "eyes" are listed below from the Douay-Rheims 1899 American Edition.

<u>Introduction of What was Heard, Seen and Touched</u>,
1 John 1:1 – 10
That which was from the beginning, which we have heard, which we have seen with our eyes, which we have looked upon, and our hands have handled, of the word of life: 1 John 1:1.

<u>The New Commandment</u>, 1 John 2:7 – 14
But he that hateth his brother, is in darkness, and walketh in darkness, and knoweth not whither he goeth; because the darkness hath blinded his eyes, 1 John 2:11.

<u>Do Not Love the World</u>, 1 John 2:15 - 17
For all that is in the world, is the concupiscence of the flesh, and the concupiscence of the eyes, and the pride of life, which is not of the Father, but is of the world, 1 John 2:16.

The Book of Revelation

Apostle John also wrote the Book of Revelation, the last book of the Bible. The Book of Revelation has 22 chapters, and it's the 66th book of the Bible. According to the Book of Revelation, John was exiled to the Island of Patmos. It was during an era when Christians were being persecuted, under the Roman Emperor Domitian. The Island of Patmos was an island in the Aegean Sea. The island was small, rocky, and barren where criminals of Rome were sent to serve out their prison sentence in harsh conditions.

According to tradition, John was deported to Patmos after being thrown into hot boiling oil in Rome and came out unharmed. On the Island of Patmos, John saw and wrote the visions described in the Book of Revelation. The word "eyes" is mentioned in 9 verses which are listed below from the American Standard Version.

<u>Christ Appears to John in A Vision</u>, Revelation 1:9 – 20
And his head and his hairs were white as white wool, white as snow; and his eyes were as a flame of fire, Revelation 1:14.

<u>The Letter to Thyatira</u>, Revelation 2:18 – 29
And to the angel of the church in Thyatira write: These things saith the Son of God, who hath his eyes like a flame of fire, and his feet are like unto burnished brass: Revelation 2:18.

The Letter to Laodicea, Revelation 3:14 – 22
I counsel thee to buy of me gold refined by fire, that thou mayest become rich; and white garments, that thou mayest clothe thyself, and that the shame of thy nakedness be not made manifest; and eyesalve to anoint thine eyes, that thou mayest see, Revelation 3:18.

Worship in Heaven, Revelation 4:1 – 11
And before the throne, as it were a sea of glass like unto crystal; and in the midst of the throne, and round about the throne, 4 living creatures full of eyes before and behind, Revelation 4:6.

And the 4 living creatures, having each one of them 6 wings, are full of eyes round about and within: and they have no rest day and night, saying, Holy, holy, holy, is the LORD God, the Almighty, who was and who is, and who is to come, Revelation 4:8.

The Slain Lamb, Revelation 5:1 – 7
And I saw in the midst of the throne and of the 4 living creatures, and in the midst of the elders, a Lamb standing, as though it had been slain, having 7 horns and 7 eyes, which are the 7 Spirits of God sent, forth into all the earth, Revelation 5:6.

The Great Crowd, Revelation 7:9 – 17
For the Lamb that is in the midst of the throne shall be their shepherd, and shall guide them unto fountains of waters of life: and God shall wipe away every tears from their eyes, Revelation 7:17.

<u>The Rider on the White Horse</u>, Revelation 19:11 – 16
And his eyes are a flame of fire, and upon his head are many diadems; and he hath a name written which no one knoweth, but he himself, Revelation 19:12.

<u>The New Heaven and the New Earth</u>, Revelation 21:1 – 27
And he shall wipe away every tears from their eyes; and death shall be no more; neither shall there be mourning, nor crying, nor pain, any more: the first things are passed away, Revelation 21:4.

A READER'S QUESTION

This new section just dropped in my spirit at 0613 on January 14, 2017, titled A Reader's Question.

An individual asked me the following question:
"How many books are you planning on writing?"

The Answer:
I really don't know.
I assume until Father God, place me on another godly assignment.

In all thy ways acknowledge him,
And he shall direct thy paths.
Proverbs 3:6 ASV

In all thy ways acknowledge him, and
he will make plain thy paths.
Proverbs 3:6 Darby

In all thy ways think on him, and
he will direct thy steps.
Proverbs 3:6 DRA

**In all your ways acknowledge him, and
he will make your paths straight.**
Proverbs 3:6 WEB

**In all thy ways acknowledge him,
and he shall direct thy paths.**
Proverbs 3:6 KJV

AUTHOR'S CLOSING REMARKS

I truly believed this book was just for me. *Smile* . . . I learnt so much, I pray you did, too. First, I discovered when you feel overwhelmed by the Lord's assignment for you; pray, fast, and seek his face for strength, instructions, and procedures. I thought the writing of this book would take over a year, but it didn't. The word "eyes" is mentioned over 500 times for various reasons and in many of the biblical events in the Bible.

Secondly, I learned that past life incidents, events, or discoveries help you with, and in your future assignments in the LORD. Even though at that present moment, you didn't fully know how that life experience would help you in your future, but the LORD did. For example, while writing the last book title: <u>Isaiah 26:3 – 4 "Perfect Peace XVIII" Midnight</u>, I ran across several other translations of the Bible that is public domain. If the LORD hadn't revealed those translations to me, this book wouldn't be possible in this format. Praise God!

Thirdly, this is the thickest book, and it took about the same number of months to compose as the other books. Hallelujah . . . Father God is *t – r – u – l – y* amazing to me! I can do all things through Christ, which strengtheneth me, Philippians 4:13 KJV. I can do all things in him that strengtheneth me, Philippians 4:13 ASV. I have strength for all things in him that gives me power, Philippians 4:13 Darby. I can do all these things in him who strengtheneth me,

Philippians 4:13 DRA. I can do all things through Christ, who strengthens me, Philippians 4:13 WEB.

I pray you will make time to read each Biblical event surrounding the word "eyes." Enjoy and let your soul be blessed in Jesus' Precious Name.

Pray for the Ministry . . . *May the "Prince of Peace," give you His Peace.*

Dr. Vanessa

REFERENCES

Chapter 1
1. BibleGateway: https://www.biblegateway.com
2. Wikipedia, The Free Encyclopedia: https://en.wikipedia.org/wiki/Eye

Chapter 2
1. BibleGateway: https://www.biblegateway.com
2. Wikipedia, The Free Encyclopedia: https://en.wikipedia.org/wiki/Moses

Chapter 3
1. BibleGateway: https://www.biblegateway.com
2. Jacksonville Theology Seminary: The Books of the Law

Chapter 4
1. BibleGateway: https://www.biblegateway.com
2. Jacksonville Theology Seminary: The Books of the Law

Chapter 5
1. BibleGateway: https://www.biblegateway.com
2. Wikipedia, The Free Encyclopedia: https://en.wikipedia.org/wiki/Book_of_Joshua
3. Jacksonville Theology Seminary: The Historical Books

Chapter 6
1. BibleGateway: https://www.biblegateway.com
2. Jacksonville Theology Seminary: The Historical Books

Chapter 7
1. BibleGateway: https://www.biblegateway.com
2. Jacksonville Theology Seminary: The Historical Books

Chapter 8
1. BibleGateway: https://www.biblegateway.com
2. Jacksonville Theology Seminary: The Historical Books

Chapter 9
1. BibleGateway: https://www.biblegateway.com
2. Jacksonville Theology Seminary: The Historical Books

Chapter 10
1. BibleGateway: https://www.biblegateway.com
2. Wikipedia, The Free Encyclopedia: https://en.wikipedia.org/wiki/Book_of_Job

Chapter 11
1. BibleGateway: https://www.biblegateway.com
2. Isaiah 26:3 – 4 "Perfect Peace XVIII" Midnight – Chapter 8

Chapter 12
1. BibleGateway: https://www.biblegateway.com
2. Wikipedia, The Free Encyclopedia: https://en.wikipedia.org/wiki/Book_of_Proverbs

Chapter 13
1. BibleGateway: https://www.biblegateway.com
2. Jacksonville Theology Seminary: Poetry and Wisdom Books of the Bible

Chapter 14
1. BibleGateway: https://www.biblegateway.com
2. Wikipedia, The Free Encyclopedia: https://en.wikipedia.org/wiki/Book_of_Isaiah

Chapter 15
1. BibleGateway: https://www.biblegateway.com
2. Jacksonville Theology Seminary: Jeremiah

Chapter 16
1. BibleGateway: https://www.biblegateway.com
2. Wikipedia, The Free Encyclopedia: https://en.wikipedia.org/wiki/Book_of_Ezekiel
3. Jacksonville Theology Seminary: Daniel

Chapter 17
1. BibleGateway: https://www.biblegateway.com
2. Wikipedia, The Free Encyclopedia: https://en.wikipedia.org/wiki/Twelve_Minor_Prophets
3. Jacksonville Theology Seminary: The Minor Prophets

Chapter 18
1. BibleGateway: https://www.biblegateway.com
2. Wikipedia, The Free Encyclopedia: https://en.wikipedia.org/wiki/Synoptic_Gospels

Chapter 19
1. BibleGateway: https://www.biblegateway.com
2. Wikipedia, The Free Encyclopedia: https://en.wikipedia.org/wiki/Acts_of_the_Apostles

Chapter 20
1. BibleGateway: https://www.biblegateway.com
2. Wikipedia, The Free Encyclopedia: https://en.wikipedia.org/wiki/Paul_the_Apostle
3. Wikipedia, The Free Encyclopedia: https://en.wikipedia.org/wiki/Epistle

Chapter 21
1. BibleGateway: https://www.biblegateway.com
2. Jacksonville Theology Seminary: Apostle Peter
3. Wikipedia, The Free Encyclopedia: https://en.wikipedia.org/wiki/Peter_the_Apostle

Chapter 22
1. BibleGateway: https://www.biblegateway.com
2. Jacksonville Theology Seminary: Apostle John
3. Wikipedia, The Free Encyclopedia: https://en.wikipedia.org/wiki/John_the_Apostle

ANSWERS & INFORMATION SECTION

Chapter 1

Formal Equivalence refers to translating by finding reasonably words and phrases that have equal value, significance or meaning while following the source language as closely as possible. This style is often referred to as "Literal Translation" or "Word-for-Word Translation"

Functional Equivalence is sometimes called "Dynamic Equivalence" or "Thought -for - Thought Translation." It is a translation process in which the translator(s) attempts to reflect and focus on the thought of the writer in the source language rather than the Word-for-Word Translation."

The extensive use of Dynamic Equivalence is called a "Paraphrase," or "Thought -for-Thought Translation." It goes even further than dynamic equivalence when translating the source. It attempts to convey some key concepts while not retaining even a dynamic equivalence with the text.

Chapter 6

<u>Who was King Josiah?</u>
King Josiah was a godly king in the eyes of the LORD. He was the son of King Amon and grandson of King Manasseh; they were both wicked kings of Judah in the eyes of the LORD.

The name Josiah means "God will save." Josiah is known as one of the youngest kings to reign. He began his reign at the age of 8 after his father, King Amon, was assassinated. Josiah reigned for 31 years, around 641 to 610 BC. Dedicated, devoted, and devout individuals guided King Josiah. They were Hilkiah, the High Priest and his son Jeremiah; Shaphan the royal scribe and his son Ahikam; Shallum the faithful chamberlain and his wife, Prophetess Huldah.

King Josiah was having the Holy Temple restored when the scroll of Moses was found. It had been hidden in a cave and lost for many generations. The High Priest Hilkiah found it and gave it to Shaphan who brought it to the king. After reading the scroll, the king sent messengers to consult with Prophetess Huldah concerning the scroll. She sent a message back to King Josiah. It told him that the LORD would bring destruction upon Israel and its inhabitants because the people have forsaken Him to serve pagan gods.

King Josiah listened to the words of the Prophetess, and like his great-grandfather Hezekiah, he purged the land of all forms of idolatry. King Josiah spread the words throughout the whole land encouraging the people to turn back to the LORD. King Josiah vowed to return the people back to the LORD. The entire population of Judah was encouraged by the King. They turned against the false priests and destroyed pagan altars that had been built across the land during the rule of the previous two kings; Amon and Manasseh.

King Josiah also re-established the Passover. The Passover is a festival celebrating Israel freedom from Egyptian bondage. Josiah was determined that this festival would serve to strengthen the relationship between Israel and the LORD, commemorating the people's return to the True and Living LORD. This Passover King Josiah had was celebrated with much sumptuousness and splendor.

The Biblical events surrounding the LORD calling names "twice" are listed below:

1. Samuel, 1 Samuel 3:10
The LORD calls to Samuel: The LORD had called Samuel 3 other times, but he thought Eli, the priest, was calling him. Eli realized that the LORD was calling Samuel. Eli told Samuel if the LORD calls him again, to say, "speak because your servant hears." The LORD came, and stood, and called "Samuel, Samuel," and Samuel answered. The LORD told Samuel, He was about to do things in Israel that would shock and surprise the people, starting with Eli and his family.

2. Abraham, Genesis 22:11
The Sacrifice of Isaac: The LORD was testing Abraham. The LORD told Abraham to take his only son to Mount Moriah to offer him as a burnt offering. Abraham built the altar, placed wood on top, bound, and laid Isaac on the altar. When Abraham reached out his hand to slay his son, the LORD's angel, shouted to Abraham from heaven, "Abraham, Abraham!" do not lay your hand on the boy. The LORD sees now; you will not withhold your son from him.

3. Jacob, Genesis 46:2
Jacob Goes to Egypt: When Joseph was about to bring his father, brothers, and their families into Egypt, the LORD spoke to Jacob in a night vision. He said, "Jacob, Jacob"

don't be afraid to go down to Egypt, for he will make him a great nation.

4.   Moses, Exodus 3:4
Moses and the Burning Bush: Moses was tending to the flock of his father-in-law, on the west side of the wilderness, near Mount Horeb. He saw from afar a burning bush that wasn't being consumed. Moses turns aside to see this sight is when the LORD called to him out of the bush, "Moses, Moses!" The LORD told Moses to take off his shoes because he was standing on holy ground and that he has seen the affliction of his people in Egypt.

5.   Martha, Luke 10:41
Jesus at the Home of Martha and Mary: Jesus was visiting with Martha and Mary. Mary chose to sit at Jesus' feet, listening to his words. Martha was distracted and busy with serving and preparing a meal. Martha asked Jesus, doesn't He care that her sister had left her to do all the work? Jesus answered Martha by calling her name twice before he told her that Mary has chosen what is better and it shall not be taken away from her.

6.   Saul, Acts 9:4
Saul's Conversion: Saul was on his journey to the synagogues in Damascus. He had orders to take believers of Jesus Christ to prison if he found any there. As he drew near to the city of Damascus, suddenly, a bright light shines about him from heaven. The LORD called Saul, Saul, why do you persecute me.

7.   Simon, Luke 22:31
The Last Supper: The LORD called Simon, name twice before he told him that Satan desires to have him and sift him like wheat.

Note of Interests: While Jesus hunged on the cross, about the 9th hour He cried out, "Eli, Eli, lama sabachthani?" in which He is saying, "My God, My God," why has thou forsaken me? Matthew 27:46 and Mark 15:34.

Chapter 16

Daniel means "God is my judge."
Hananiah means "Beloved of the LORD."
Mishael means "Who is as God."
Azariah means "The Lord is my Help."

Chapter 20

Paul greets by name 27 people in a congregation he had never visited, and they are listed below.

1. Phoebe, a deacon in the church at Cenchrea
2. Prisca
3. Aquila
4. Epaenetus, the 1st convert to Messiah in Asia
5. Mary
6. Andronicus
7. Junia
8. Ampliatus
9. Urbanus
10. Stachys
11. Apelles
12. Aristobulus and family
13. Herodion
14. Narcissus and family

15. Tryphaena
16. Tryphosa
17. Persis
18. Rufus and his mother
19. Asyncritus
20. Phlegon
21. Hermes
22. Patrobas
23. Hermas and the brothers who are with them
24. Philologus
25. Julia
26. Nereus and his sister
27. Olympas and all the saints who are with them

<u>The Epistles of Paul which doesn't contain the word "eyes."</u>
1 Corinthians
2 Corinthians
Philippians
Colossians
1 Thessalonians
2 Thessalonians
1 Timothy
2 Timothy
Titus
Philemon

Chapter 21

No.	The 37 Miracles of Jesus	Matthew	Mark	Luke	John
1	Jesus Turns Water to Wine				2:1-11
2	Jesus Heals an Official's Son				4:43-54

No.		Matthew	Mark	Luke	John
3	Jesus Drives Out an Evil Spirit		1:21:27	4:31-36	
4	Jesus Heals Peter's Mother-in-Law	8:14-15	1:29-31	4:38-39	
5	Jesus Heals Many Sick at Evening	8:16-17	1:32-34	4:40-41	
6	1st Miraculous Catch of Fish			5:1-11	
7	Jesus Cleans a Man with Leprosy	8:1-4	1:40-45	5:12-14	
8	Jesus Heals a Centurion's Servant	8:5-13		7:1-10	
9	Jesus Heals a Paralytic	9:1-8	2:1-12	5:17-26	
No.		Matthew	Mark	Luke	John
10	Jesus Heals a Man's Withered Hand	12:9-14	3:1-6	6:6-11	
11	Jesus Raises a Widow's Son from the Dead in Nain			7:11-17	
12	Jesus Calms a Storm	8:23-27	4:35-41	8:22-25	
13	Jesus Casts Demons Out of a Man into a Herd of Pigs	8:28-33	5:1-20	8:26-39	
14	Jesus Heals a Woman in the Crowd	9:20-22	5:25-34	8:42-48	
15	Jesus Raises Jairus' Daughter	9:18-26	5:21-43	8:40-56	

No.		Matthew	Mark	Luke	John
16	Jesus Heals 2 Blind Men	9:27-31			
17	Jesus Heals a Mute Man	9:32-34			
18	Jesus Heals a Lame Man at Bethesda				5:1-15
19	Jesus Feeds 5,000	14:13-21	6:30-44	9:10-17	6:1-15
20	Jesus Walks on Water	14:22-33	6:45-52		6:16-2121
21	Jesus Heals Many Sick in Gennesaret	14:34-36	6:53-56		
22	Jesus Heals a Gentile Woman's Demon-Possessed Daughter	5:21-28	7:24-30		
23	Jesus Heals a Deaf and Dumb Man		7:31-37		
24	Jesus Feeds 4,000	15:32-39	8:1-13		
25	Jesus Heals a Blind Man at Bethsaida		8:22-26		
26	Jesus Heals a Man Born Blind				9:1-12
27	Jesus Heals a Boy with a Demon	17:14-20	9:14-29	9:37-43	
28	Miraculous Temple Tax in a Fish Mouth	17:24-27			
No.		Matthew	Mark	Luke	John
29	Jesus Heals a Blind, Mute, Demon Oppressed Man	12:22-23		11:14-23	

30	Jesus Heals a Crippled Woman			13:10-17	
31	Jesus Heals a Man with Dropsy			14:1-6	
32	Jesus Cleanses 10 Lepers			17:11-19	
33	Jesus Raises Lazarus from the Dead				11:1-45
34	Jesus Restores Sight to Bartimaeus	20:29-34	10:46-52	18:35-43	
35	Jesus Withers the Fig Tree	21:18-22	11:12-14		
36	Jesus Heals a Malchus Severed Ear by Peter			22:50-51	
37	2nd Miraculous Catch of Fish				21:4-11

OTHER BOOKS BY THE AUTHOR

From the Pew to the Pulpit — Published: 08/29/2007

Isaiah 26:3-4 "Perfect Peace" — Published: 09/16/2010*

Isaiah 26:3-4 "Perfect Peace" The Last Single Digit — Published: 02/15/2012*

Isaiah 26:3-4 "Perfect Peace III" Silver and Gold — Published: 10/29/2012*

Isaiah 26:3-4 "Perfect Peace IV" The Kingdom Number — Published: 04/15/2013*

Isaiah 26:3-4 "Perfect Peace V" 2541 — Published: 09/13/2013*

Isaiah 26:3-4 "Perfect Peace VI" Zacchaeus — Published: 02/28/2014

Isaiah 26:3-4 "Perfect Peace VII" Eleven — Published: 10/30/2014*

Isaiah 26:3-4 "Perfect Peace VIII" Prayer — Published: 05/21/2015*

Isaiah 26:3-4 "Perfect Peace IX" Sixteen — Published: 10/24/2015*

Isaiah 26:3-4 "Perfect Peace X" Dreams — Published: 04/12/2016

Isaiah 26:3-4 "Perfect Peace XI" Door — Published: 02/13/2017

Isaiah 26:3-4 "Perfect Peace XII" River — Published: 08/02/2017

Isaiah 26:3-4 "Perfect Peace XIII" 1 Kings 19:1-18 — Published: 12/18/2017

Isaiah 26:3-4 "Perfect Peace XIV" G – Men — Published: 05/03/2018*

Isaiah 26:3-4 "Perfect Peace XV" 11:29 — Published: 07/26/2018

Isaiah 26:3-4 "Perfect Peace XVI" Shoes — Published: 10/31/2018*

Isaiah 26:3-4 "Perfect Peace XVII" Arrow — Published: 01/25/2019*

Isaiah 26:3-4 "Perfect Peace XVIII" Midnight — Published: 04/26/2019

PS: On 5/25/2019, I noticed that some of the book published dates vary slightly from AuthorHouse, depending on which bookstore site you visit. They have been modified to reflect AuthorHouse's publication date, indicated by an *.

Printed in the United States
By Bookmasters